Murderous
EAST ANGLIA

Murderous EAST ANGLIA

Casting a Flickering Candle over a Miscellany of Dark and Nefarious Deeds Resulting in Bloodshed

JOANNA ELPHICK

authorHOUSE®

AuthorHouse™ UK
1663 Liberty Drive
Bloomington, IN 47403 USA
www.authorhouse.co.uk
Phone: 0800.197.4150

© 2015 Joanna Elphick. All rights reserved.

No part of this book may be reproduced, stored in a retrieval system, or transmitted by any means without the written permission of the author.

Published by AuthorHouse 06/11/2015

ISBN: 978-1-5049-4409-0 (sc)
ISBN: 978-1-5049-4412-0 (e)

Print information available on the last page.

Any people depicted in stock imagery provided by Thinkstock are models, and such images are being used for illustrative purposes only. Certain stock imagery © Thinkstock.

This book is printed on acid-free paper.

Because of the dynamic nature of the Internet, any web addresses or links contained in this book may have changed since publication and may no longer be valid. The views expressed in this work are solely those of the author and do not necessarily reflect the views of the publisher, and the publisher hereby disclaims any responsibility for them.

Contents

A Brief Introduction vii

Chapter 1: A Death at Providence House 1
Chapter 2: The Butcher of Norwich 15
Chapter 3: Spade Work 24
Chapter 4: A Death in the Old Red Barn 29
Chapter 5: When Love Goes Wrong, Nothing Goes Right 41
Chapter 6: In The Blood 49
Chapter 7: The Bootlace Beach Murder 51
Chapter 8: Battered For the Last Time 57
Chapter 9: The Stanfield Hall Slayings 62
Chapter 10: A Duel to the Death on Cawston Heath 75
Chapter 11: Who Should Hang for the Death of Mrs Candler? 83
Chapter 12: The Landlord of the Lamb 90
Chapter 13: The Abominable Sins of the Tailor of Diss 93
Chapter 14: Marriage, Madness, Murder & Suicide 99
Chapter 15: The Last Dance of Louie Bryant 105
Chapter 16: All's Well That Ends Well 108
Chapter 17: And So to Bed… 113

A Final Thank You 117

A Brief Introduction

Welcome to East Anglia, a breathtakingly beautiful area famous for its vast skies, picturesque villages and meandering waterways teeming with wildlife. What a magnificent place in which to reside; a place to bring up children, take long walks hand in hand with the one you love and potter through your twilight years... or is it?

The counties of Norfolk and Suffolk fulfill many people's dream of the perfect getaway, however it may well come as quite a shock to discover that there are more suspicious deaths per capita in East Anglia than in central London. So what is it about this glorious part of the country that leads ordinary folk to such savage and unbridled behaviour?

This book considers such questions whilst discussing some of the most fascinating tales occurring in the region. Pertinent legal points that are raised will be examined and set in historical context. So join me as I journey through the darker realms of East Anglia and meet an array of executioners, poisoners, cutthroats, wayward farmers and saucy young maids.

You will learn of the craft and eventual abolition of capital punishment, the changing laws regarding arsenic and the development of forensic detection. Hopefully your imaginations will be inflamed and you may well wish to discover more, so, with this in mind, there are many pointers throughout the book showing you where to go to visit these places for yourself.

Now, let us linger no longer in the sunlight but plunge into the stygian shadows of Murderous East Anglia.

Chapter 1

A Death at Providence House

It was a dark and stormy night... what a wonderful way in which to start a torrid story of lust, betrayal and, ultimately, murder, but that is exactly how one should begin the sorry tale of poor Rose Harsent.

The storm that broke on Saturday 31st May 1902 was the worst in living memory. The day time had been unbearably hot and sultry. Early evening brought the first heavy raindrops and by nightfall lightning flashed across the sweeping skies of East Anglia, illuminating the village of Peasenhall. Saturday night and Sunday morning was the outcome of a raging, uncontrollable weather front, but it was also the culmination of another furious and inevitable explosion, one resulting not in thunder but in homicide.

Rose Harsent was a rather pretty twenty-three year old maid, working for one Mr and Mrs Crisp with whom she resided at Providence House. As well as cooking and cleaning for Mrs Georgina Crisp, young Rose took it upon herself to help clean the local Methodist church, known as the Doctor's Chapel, where her mistress was a member of the congregation. Rose was not a Congregationalist herself but, being an astute woman, realized that it was here, behind the chapel door, that security and a future within the village could be obtained. How ironic then that it should be behind this very Chapel door that Rose's problems should begin.

William Gardiner was the archetypal hero of the day: tall, dark-haired and handsome. As choirmaster, Assistant Steward and Sunday-School Teacher to the village children, thirty-four year old William had a flourishing future under the auspices of the Chapel. He supported his loving wife and six children by working as foreman at the local drill works owned by Smythe & Sons, where he oversaw the manufacture of agricultural equipment for the local farming community. His star, as they say, was in the ascension, for no man had a greater reputation in Peasenhall. It was an impressive place in which William should find himself since he was no local and his past was distinctly mysterious. Had the Primitive Methodists cared to question the birthdays of their offspring they may well have discovered that the arrival of their eldest daughter did not quite tally with the date of their marriage. But luckily for the Gardiners, they were taken at face value, a fine upstanding family led by a strong and honourable father. Yes, William was indeed quite the gentleman, even if young Georgina Gardiner's father had cut her off without a penny for marrying so far beneath her.

The young and impressionable Rose was mightily impressed with the fine figure cut by Mr William Gardiner. He in turn was more than a little pleased to take time out of his busy life to teach her to play the church organ, encouraging her to join the choir and even convince her to help him run the Chapel Sunday School. No surprise, then, that malicious rumours soon began to spread through the village.

Things came to a head on 1st May 1901. Two good-for-nothing lads -George Wright, who worked with Gardiner at the drill works, and his friend Alphonso Skinner - were wandering along the path back into the village when they noticed Rose walking purposefully the other way, heading towards the Doctor's Chapel. For no apparent reason the two boys hid in the early evening shadows, watching her as she slipped through the Chapel door. Before they could creep up on their unsuspecting victim another trod the path down to the Methodist dwelling. William Gardiner was clearly seen entering the Chapel, closing the door firmly behind him.

Although both Rose and William had every right to be in the Chapel on that warm May evening, George and Alphonso were suitably intrigued and decided to investigate further. Imagine their surprise on listening at the door and hearing the muffled giggles and whispers of a pair up to no good. The fine upstanding William Gardiner was clearly teaching young Rose more than how to play the organ - chapel organ that is...

The two lads took no time in spreading the saucy news and it was a mere two days later that an enquiry was set up by the Methodist chapel superintendent, one Mr John Guy. William faced the religious panel dowsed in humiliation. Of course he had a spotless reputation to lean upon but the fact that both Wright and Skinner repeatedly refused to recant their sordid tale put serious doubt into the minds of the God-fearing congregation. William's story of a jammed chapel door swollen by the damp seemed a curious explanation, but neither his nor the boys' tale could be verified and it soon became clear that there would be no perfect conclusion to the situation. As a result, foetid rumours hung in the air as a malodorous, unwanted fish on a plate might until it is swept into the rubbish. William was not, strictly speaking, guilty of anything, but he felt obliged to walk away from the various Methodist posts he had worked so very hard to acquire. His pregnant wife, Georgina, had no option but to publicly stand by her husband, a position she would be required to return to later on whilst an embarrassed Rose dusted and polished the Chapel with religious fervour in an attempt to redeem her sullied character. Sadly, Georgina eventually succumbed to the stress and humiliation of her husband's supposed indiscretions; her seventh child was stillborn.

After a while things returned to normal in the quiet village of Peasenhall. William gradually rebuilt his reputation and to all intents and purpose behaved as the dutiful, attentive husband. Work flourished and his position at the chapel was reinstated. Occasionally William was seen in animated conversation with Rose but there was no harm in pleasantries and any suspicion was generally disregarded. However, all past accusations would soon be remembered and shared with far more than the local community.

The night of Saturday 31st May was, as previously mentioned, an unholy wild one. Lightning flashed across the sky and lit up the villagers, who stood in their doorways watching the violent weather front unfold. The timings and whereabouts of William Gardiner throughout the storm were of vital importance during the subsequent trials but exact details were never fully established. It was known that he returned home from a trip to nearby Kelsale at approximately nine o'clock and a neighbour distinctly remembered chatting outside Gardiner's cottage at ten because he had noticed a light flickering in an upper window of Providence House, and was surprised by it at such a late hour. Further evidence propounded in court clearly showed both William and Georgina spent the majority of that fateful night with their nearby neighbour, Mrs Dickinson. Unfortunately for William, his wife admitted that, although they were together during the storm until about 1.30 Sunday morning when they returned home, William arrived after Georgina, thereby allowing a clear window of opportunity to slip away. It did not help Gardiner's defence that it was during this period where William was unaccounted for that Mrs Crisp reported hearing a loud thud downstairs at Providence House. Her husband believed it to be a clap of thunder and told his wife to try to get back to sleep. She would later find the exact time difficult to recall.

Of course the truly horrible events of Saturday night were not to be discovered until Sunday morning. The storm eventually subsided and the people of Peasenhall were beginning to rebuild fences, pull down the sand bags and

Joanna Elphick

check on the livestock. All was calm once again as William Harsent trundled through the Conservatory of Providence House to bring his daughter some freshly ironed clothes. At eight o'clock precisely Mr Harsent walked into the kitchen and stumbled across the mutilated, bloody corpse of his once beautiful child. Rose lay at the foot of the stairs. Her throat had been cut, severing the windpipe and sending a fountain of blood across the room. Two further gashes ripped into her body in a savage display of animalistic violence whilst her hands were a patchwork of cuts. Her nightdress was singed by the candle she had been carrying and had dropped as her assailant leapt out at her. An oil lamp had also been knocked over adding gasoline to the gagging smell of blood and burnt cloth. Clearly more than the storm had raged during the previous night.

A shocked William Harsent was taken away whilst the local constable, PC Nunn, arrived to investigate. Little could be gleaned from the murder site itself; clearly Rose had been ambushed at the bottom of the stairs and had put up quite a struggle before the death blow across the wind pipe had been struck. The burnt nightgown was the result of the startled maid dropping her candle and setting fire to herself, but as to who committed the heinous act, there were no clues. However, up in her bedroom, PC Nunn found three notes, one of which was to become enormously important as the trial progressed. Two letters were penned by William Gardiner but PC Nunn saw little relevance since they were both written months before. A cannier policeman might have asked himself why Rose would have kept such innocuous notes unless they held a more personal meaning to her but Nunn disregarded them and they were only brought forward at the trial to compare the handwriting with that of the third and most scintillating correspondence. This mysterious note was unsigned and concerned the final hours of Rose.

Bizarrely, the initial proposition was one of suicide, but this was quickly disregarded when the doctor pointed out it would be most difficult to stab yourself twice and then slit your own throat from right to left. No, this was clearly foul play, but who was to blame? It was at this point that the name of William Gardiner was raised. Wright and Skinner were once again the centre of attention as they relived the 'Chapel Door Incident'. Coupled with the letters found in Rose's bedroom, William was beginning to look mightily suspicious to the locals.

As was the custom of the day, an inquest into the death of Ms Harsent was held at a nearby Inn. The *Swan* became a hive of activity as villagers jostled on the path outside, waiting for the latest instalment. One can only imagine the reaction when it was announced that, not only was Rose dead (no great shock there) but also that she had been six months pregnant on the night of her murder.

A mere three days after the gruesome discovery Gardiner was arrested. A series of hearings at Saxmundham Magistrates court followed which can only be described as farcical. The use of evidence ranged from being totally overlooked to blown out of all proportion. Ultimately, the jury had decided William Gardiner was the killer and he was frogmarched back into custody to await a formal trial at the following Ipswich Assizes.

On 7th November 1902 William Gardiner faced the court for the first time. As the trial unfolded it soon became clear

Joanna Elphick

that the Defence, a young Mr Ernest Wild, was rather out of his depth. Counsel for the Prosecution, on the other hand, was none other than Mr Henry Dickens (son of Charles no less!), a superb barrister and eloquent advocate.

Weak, circumstantial evidence was paraded before the jury, who were clearly awestruck by the experienced Mr Dickens. All, that is, except one. As the trial drew to a close some three days later, the jury returned a verdict of guilty eleven to one. Luckily for William, majority verdicts were not acceptable at the time and the shaken accused was led back to the cells to await a second trial.

Christmas must have been a very bleak one for an exhausted William Gardiner, who was not led back into the dock until Wednesday 21st January. Both Wild and Dickens resumed their roles and whilst the events reached their dramatic climax, outside the County Hall at Ipswich the public were in a positive frenzy. The trial was quite simply a sensation.

The sordid events surrounding the Doctor's Chapel were re-introduced. Gossip was laid before the jury in the form of Wright and Skinner, who were brought forward to testify. They did not waver from their original story.

Mrs Crisp tried in vain to establish the exact time that the onerous 'thud' was heard during the great storm but unfortunately she could only reduce the time to between one and two in the morning. Half an hour either way could have secured Gardiner's guilt or innocence but, frustratingly, neither barrister could sway her.

Dramatic new evidence manifested itself in the form of a small, broken bottle found beside the body by PC Nunn.

A label tied about the neck of the bottle showed the dosage instructions for a child's medicine. The name upon the label…Mrs Gardiner. This fortuitous piece of evidence was greedily grasped by Mr Dickens and flourished before the jury but all was not lost for William Gardiner. As Mrs Georgina Gardiner took to the stand she calmly explained that the bottle had been given to Rose after she had decanted some camphorated oil into it. This explanation appeared to have been readily accepted by the jury but it does seem rather unlikely that Mrs Gardiner should be helping out the woman who had partially caused the death of her unborn child only a year ago.

Of course the most exciting evidence was the mysterious note found up in Rose's bedroom, relating to the night of the murder. The jury listened intently as the all too telling letter was read out.

I will try to see you tonight at 12 o'clock at your place if you put a light in your window at 10 o'clock for about ten minutes then you can take it out again, don't have a light in your room at 12 as I will come round to the back.

Here was the trap, the snare that was to bring about the ghastly end of young Rose Harsent and it left the jury momentarily stunned. This was no sudden, passionate argument that ended in bloodshed. This was a cold, premeditated plan to do away with an irritating problem, a problem that was carrying an unborn child and was bubbling with a future that could never be.

She had set the light at ten o'clock as instructed. If you remember, a neighbour had chatted to William about a flickering candle in the top window of Providence House.

She had clearly known who had sent her the note since there was no signature, and yet she had willingly complied with its contents. She had waited for her lover to arrive, tip-toeing down the stairs at the given hour only to be met by death.

The 'how' was obvious, but the 'who' was less so. Somebody had been having an affair with Rose right under the noses of the God-fearing community. However, news of an unwanted pregnancy had clearly put an enormous strain on the relationship. One more assignation was required to end the affair for good, but who was it? Rose had been a very pretty girl with numerous admirers. Was the jury certain that it was Gardiner who had slit her throat and left her to bleed to death at the foot of her mistress' stairs? Or was it another who had led her astray? She was clearly not the virginal maid she had maintained to be throughout her short life. The jury were baffled, confused but most importantly, unsure of the evidence that had been offered to them.

On 24th January 1903, a red-faced Foreman stood before the judge, the Honourable Sir John Compton Lawrence, and admitted that, once again, the jury were undecided - eleven to one but this time in favour of the defendant. The court was in an uproar as William Gardiner sank down into his chair, shaking uncontrollably and covering his face with his shackled hands. How much longer would this nightmare continue?

In truth, it would not be long. Five days later the Director of Public Prosecutions announced that a third trial would not be taking place and a deeply relieved William was immediately released.

Murderous East Anglia

Nobody else was ever indicted for the murder of Rose Harsent. The villagers gradually returned to their parochial business whilst the Gardiners left Peasenhall for good and were not heard of again. Various stories grew up as to their whereabouts but none can be confirmed.

So, did justice prevail, allowing a good Christian man to go free, or did William Gardiner evade the noose on a technicality and literally get away with murder? Like many a fine murderous melodrama that begins with 'It was a dark and stormy night' the end is shrouded in mystery…

The final resting place of Rose Harsent

Legal Ponderings - Juries

Possibly the most important point to mention at this juncture is the fact that, unlike today's trials, in 1903 a court was required to deliver a unanimous verdict in order to obtain a conviction. Majority verdicts would not be introduced until 1st October 1967 under the Criminal Justice Act. This was further advanced under section 17 of The Juries Act 1974 which states:

...the verdict of a jury in proceedings in the Crown Court or the High Court need not be unanimous if:

(a) In a case where there are not less than eleven jurors, ten of them agree on the verdict: and

(b) In a case where there are ten jurors, nine of them agree on the verdict.

No court shall accept a verdict unless it appears to the court that the jury have had such period of time for deliberation as the court thinks reasonable having regard to the nature and complexity of the case; and the Crown shall in any event not accept such a verdict unless it appears to the court that the jury have had at least two hours for deliberation.

Clearly this was due to the finality of the punishment. Until capital punishment was abolished in 1968, unanimous verdicts would be required during a homicide trial. The need for a unanimous verdict was obviously of vital significance to William Gardiner since a majority verdict would have seen him hang.

You may well be wondering what occurred between the first trial and the second to completely reverse the outcome from eleven to one in favour of the prosecution to eleven to one against. The facts are extremely interesting and led to a second legal point that plagues the court trials of today.

Whilst waiting for the second trial, Mrs Gardiner took it upon herself to write a letter to the *Times* newspaper, in which she poured her heart out, explaining how desperate things had become at home for her and their children. The initial trial had gained enormous countrywide publicity and as a result everybody wanted to be involved. Donations flooded in along with letters of condolence for the poor Gardiner family. On publication of the shamelessly sentimental letter from Georgina, the *East Anglian Daily Times* decided to run with a similar article of 'Save the Gardiner Children'. Imagine the effects of such support upon the second trial jury members. Sympathy had already been firmly planted into their minds, weighing heavy on their hearts. Whatever will happen to the children if we find William Gardiner guilty? Georgina had cleverly humanized her husband and pushed his family to centre stage.

The evidence was, if anything, slightly more damning at the second trial with the release of the medicine bottle although, if truth be told, none of it amounted to more than circumstantial evidence and yet William was found almost entirely innocent. If ever there was proof of the effects of media interference, this was it.

When gathering a jury for trial, the judge must ensure a complete lack of bias. No previous knowledge is allowed but in reality how can this possibly be? Imagine the difficulty faced by the American courts as they struggled to find a jury for the Michael Jackson paedophilia charges - Do you know the defendant? Do you have any preconceived ideas relating to the defendant? There are few people on this planet who could answer in the negative resulting in repeated claims of an unconstitutional trial for the 'King of Pop'.

The continual interference of the press causes enormous problems for the courts but this is obviously not a modern phenomenon as seen during the Gardiner trials.

Chapter 2

The Butcher of Norwich

Guilt is a dreadful emotion, gnawing away at the very soul, maintaining a healthy pulse in the heart of past indiscretions whilst destroying any hope of a productive future. No one knew this to be true more than one Mr William Sheward, a man whose guilty mind literally led him to the gallows.

In 1836 William, a twenty-four year old pawnbroker's assistant, married thirty-eight year old Martha Francis in London where they both worked. Times were extremely hard for the Shewards and so it wasn't long before they moved back to East Anglia where Martha originated from. To begin with they stayed in Wymondham with Martha's sister Mary, but the town, although cheaper than London, held few job prospects.

William took it upon himself to move his new wife once again, but this time to Norwich where he hoped employment opportunities might improve. They didn't.

Joanna Elphick

Money, or to be more precise, a lack of money, was to be a constant issue within the marriage. William trekked from job to job in an endless bid to please his wife but to no avail. Financially, the Shewards were a mess. If the couple were not arguing about money, Martha was complaining about her husband's interest in younger women. The marriage was an unmitigated disaster. In 1849 a bankrupt William gave up on his dream of becoming an independent tailor and took a job working for a dubious Norwich pawnbroker by the name of Mr Christie. The two men appeared to get on extremely well, so much so in fact that William's new boss even agreed to look after £400 of the Shewards' money so that the creditors would not be able to get their hands on it. A combination of their newfound friendship and their weekly business jaunts to Great Yarmouth proved too much for Martha, who spent the majority of her time complaining, arguing and generally moaning about her lot. The £400 savings finding their way into Mr Christie's hands proved to be the last straw.

Saturday 14st June was hot and sticky. As Martha ranted about the money and the fact that her husband was, once again, leaving her at home whilst he sloped off to Great Yarmouth, William finally lost the remnants of his patience. With an unnatural quickness, William bounded across the room, stopping inches from her face, where he sliced into her throat with a razor. The carotid artery gaped wide and a fountain of blood sprayed the walls and splashed the floor. William calmly stood over the body of his now silent wife and gazed into the fireplace mirror. His hair dripped crimson. Without a moment's hesitation he slipped back into the bedroom, washed his face and changed his clothes. Within ten minutes he had locked the front door and was on his way to keep his meeting in Great Yarmouth. Martha no longer cared. Her lifeless corpse, now silent, lay in a crumpled heap as the blood began to seep into the rug beneath her.

On his return, William was faced with a rather cumbersome dilemma. Whatever was he to do with Martha? Clearly he needed to get rid of her, but how he chose to accomplish this remains one of the most gruesome tales to emanate from East Anglia.

First of all, he chopped off her head and placed it in a pot of boiling water. He then proceeded to remove the hands and feet, adding them to the bubbling concoction on the stove. The next few days were extremely busy for William, who spent his days working in the City and his nights cutting Martha up into manageable chunks. The June summer remained hot and humid, aggravating the unbearable stench of congealing blood, putrid flesh and cooking limbs. William burnt lavender day and night in an attempt to keep the gagging smell at bay but to no avail. Eventually the boiling stage was abandoned. It was both time-consuming and smelly. When all was said and done, Martha had to go. A few days after the crime, William began to take nightly jaunts through the back streets of Norwich, carrying a slop bucket filled with flesh. Fingers and toes were liberally flung behind hedges, chunks of putrid meat were stuffed in fox holes, Martha's flaming red hair was thrown to the wind and her entrails were surreptitiously poured down the drains. The head was never discovered - one can only imagine where he offloaded it. A putrefying hand was dropped proudly at the feet of one poor dog-walker by a frisky Cocker Spaniel, and a pair of school children stumbled across a number of digits whilst playing in a nearby coppice.

Joanna Elphick

Strange as it may seem, nobody was overly concerned to begin with. The liberal sprinkling of body parts was put down to medical students playing a gruesome prank. And as for poor old Martha, no one was surprised when William announced that his long-suffering wife had upped and left him for an old flame, with the unlikely name of Worseldine, in New Zealand. William appeared to be off the hook. As the 1851 Christmas festivities unfolded, the un-named body parts were laid to rest under a covering of lime in the basement of the Guildhall in Norwich.

The house at Tabernacle Street was scrupulously scrubbed, scoured, swabbed and swept until every last oozing drop of blood had vanished, along with Mr Sheward, who scuttled off to find new digs in nearby Kings Street. Financially, things began to look somewhat rosier. Girlfriends came and went until he met a young girl by the name of Charlotte Buck. Through hazy, drunken eyes Charlotte seemed to be the answer to his prayers. She quickly moved in with him and over the course of nine years they raised three children. Eventually the pair married but things were beginning to fall apart for William. Having left the security of Mr Christie's employ, Sheward had attempted to work for himself in the pawnbrokers business. This venture failed so he moved his family to Oak Street where he became the landlord of the *Key and Castle Tavern*.

Leaving a drunk in charge of a public house proved to be an unwise decision. William drank away the profits, sitting up long after closing time until he collapsed on the floor. Charlotte, meanwhile, became increasingly frightened by his drunken ramblings about his dead wife chopped up and left to rot throughout Norwich. William was beginning to unravel but he was not the only one with morbid thoughts and nagging worries.

Mary, Martha's twin, was deeply concerned that she had not heard from her beloved sister. Doubts began to fret away and her mind wandered back to the time her sister first disappeared. Just as Martha vanished, body parts began to surface including, Mary recalled, hands, feet and entrails. Although no head had ever been discovered, one woman had complained that ginger hair had covered her washing hanging out to dry. Mary only had to close her eyes and memories of a copper-headed Martha appeared. Daily articles of gruesome finds filled the local paper. Could William be guilty of such a maleficent crime? Initially her husband warned her to leave well alone but when a distant relative passed away, leaving Martha an inheritance of £300, Mary felt obliged to trace her sister and let her know. After all, last time they had met Martha had commented on their considerable money worries.

Sheward, meanwhile, was rapidly spiralling out of control. He had gotten away with a brutal, heinous act but his mind had clearly not forgiven or forgotten. Christmas 1868 was the last straw for a fragile William. As the children played and Charlotte's family congratulated their daughter on finding a husband with steady employment, William began to crumple beneath the joyous hullabaloo. Suicide appeared to be the only option left. On 29th December, William slipped out of the back door of the *Key and Castle* with his cutthroat razor and took the first available train to London.

It was here in the hustle and bustle of Walworth that he had first met Martha. Happy memories filled his head and guilt finally caught up with him. He may have avoided the law but there was no escaping his conscience now it had been unleashed.

On New Year's Eve, William staggered into Carter Street Police Station and finally unburdened his soul to a young and rather startled officer. Initially the policeman laughed the confession off as the ramblings of a drunken reveller but something in Sheward's demeanour unsettled the sergeant. Having contacted the Norfolk police station, it was confirmed that female body parts had indeed been discovered around the time of the alleged murder. A woman had also been in complaining that her sister, one Martha Sheward, had disappeared. William was immediately taken into custody and charged with Murder.

The feeble wreck of a man, labelled the Butcher of Norwich, was finally committed to the Norwich Assizes where his trial was set for 29th March. When the two-day hearing finally arrived it quickly became a frenzied affair. The visitor's gallery overflowed whilst the streets outside the court house were blocked with onlookers. Reporters pushed and shoved for a glimpse of the infamous wife mutilator as twenty-five witnesses were secretly ushered in through a side entrance.

Whatever the media circus was waiting for, they were certainly not expecting the puny, crippled old man, riddled with rheumatism that had to be carried into the dock. What a disappointment! However, the bloodthirsty and the morbid were soon reeling at the gruesome tale as it unfolded under oath. Ladies swooned, eyes grew wide and skin blanched as the last moments of Martha Sheward's life were vividly reconstructed. Reporters salaciously described William's night time forays, overflowing bucket in hand and hack saw at the ready, causing newspapers to fly off the stands. Meanwhile, savvy street vendors sold smelling salts to the delicate ladies as they staggered out of the court.

It did not take the jury long to come to a unanimous decision. William Sheward was clearly guilty of this most heinous crime despite his pitiful appearance in the dock. The old man didn't seem to care. He had been sentenced to a lifetime of torment from the moment his guilty mind had caught up with him. The death sentence was duly passed and the wardens carried him back to the cells.

On Tuesday 20th April, William Sheward's whispering conscience was finally silenced by the infamous hands of William Calcraft. Martha's remains were disturbed for the last time as the Guildhall basement was dug up and the bones removed to a quiet nearby cemetery where her beloved sister Mary could visit her regularly.

Legal Ponderings - Face of a Killer

The public's reaction to such vile behaviour is highly interesting, but what is truly fascinating is the impact of the real man as opposed to the monster in our minds. The onlookers could only imagine what a brutal wife killer who had savagely hacked and ripped away at his spouse's body could look like.

During the early nineteenth century, the police and psychiatrists alike believed that such cruel and bestial behaviour would show itself in the facial features - bulging eyes, hunched shoulders, snarling lips. Some thirty-eight years later, the same mistake would be made as grotesque caricatures of Jack the Ripper were printed in every newspaper. Whilst the public and police were on the lookout for a freak of nature staggering through the dark alleyways of Whitechapel, a seemingly normal psychopath slipped by unnoticed.

To some extent this mistake is still made today. Whilst a killer remains anonymous we imagine monsters walking among us. How disappointing then, when the murderer is caught and appears to be no different from you or I; a bearded lorry driver named Peter Sutcliffe, a quiet librarian named Dennis Neilson, a solitary neighbour called Fred West.

The reaction of the public when William Sheward staggered into the Docks was particularly shocking. Whilst they were truly appalled at the level of barbarity involved, they could not accept that this was the work of the wizened old man standing before them. The evidence was overwhelming - he was undeniably guilty, giving two confessions across the course of the trial and execution eradicating any potential doubt, but still the public were uneasy.

Many felt he had suffered enough, what with his agonizing rheumatism and crippling guilt. A petition was created and sent around Norwich begging for his release. Amazingly, over five hundred bleeding souls signed it. The courts, however, were unmoved.

Knowing the crushing guilty conscience Sheward carried on his feeble shoulders, perhaps a reprieve would have been a harsher punishment than the long drop? Either way, our psyche remains unprepared to accept the ordinary can harbour such malignity.

A new housing estate now stands on the site of the tavern.

Chapter 3

Spade Work

We all do things in the heat of the moment, say things we shouldn't, take things we know we have no right to take… it is quite simply human nature. Panic, of course, can lead us along a very dubious trail of regret, but hopefully no one reading this tale would cling so vigorously to the wrong path as one John Self.

In 1841, Wymondham was a pretty rural town with a strong sense of community and a low crime rate. Apple scrumping and drunken sing-songs were the biggest problems. It was within these idyllic surroundings that Jemima Stimpson played. She was a beautiful girl, already turning heads but still innocent enough to not look out of place laughing and running with the other children.

John Self was a little older and far less innocent. He had watched Jemima from a distance on numerous occasions but never ventured too near; after all she was very young. However, on 17th July 1841, fate found them walking together along the same path. Self engaged the girl in conversation, finding her a happy, willing companion. Misconstruing her giggling demeanour, he lunged at her, ripping her skirt in the process. The assault was quick but terrifying for Jemima, who tried to run away. Self followed, catching her by the wrists and begging her not to tell anyone. He apologized for scaring her and swore he would never touch her again if she would just keep his actions a secret. Jemima was having none of it. She pushed the panicking man backwards calling over her shoulder that her mother would hear of it.

John, late for work, ran back to town but found his mind wandering to Jemima and, more importantly, her furious mother. He picked up his spade and left. On the way home he was relieved to see Jemima throwing stones into the river. Clearly she had not been home yet. Once again he begged her to keep quiet, promising her treats if she forgot all about it. Jemima, however, was not to be bought. As she adamantly shook her head and turned to leave, John Self finally lost his temper. Swinging the spade above his head he cracked the tool against the base of her skull. Her bonnet flew off and the girl sank briefly to her knees before falling face first in the mud.

Joanna Elphick

Down by the 'Tiffy', Wymondham

John dragged her up by her pinafore and hurled her into the river like a discarded ragdoll. The wind had caught the bonnet and it was now dancing down the lane towards the village. Pulling himself through the muddy riverbank, Self raced after the incriminating evidence before returning to pick up the murder weapon.

Imagine the horror as Self returned, only to find the unstoppable Jemima Stimpson staggering out of the river! Yet another opportunity to make amends showed itself to the hot-headed youth and, yet again, that opportunity was ignored. With furious determination Self lunged at the girl, hitting her once more around the back of the head but this time holding her down with the tip of the spade until her lifeless corpse stopped fighting for breath.

Had young Jemima Stimpson told her mother of the rather pathetic assault, John Self would probably have served a minor sentence, possibly no more than a slap round the ear by the parson. Now, however, he faced the noose. His execution on 14th August was sent out as a warning to other temper-fuelled youths who thought they could abuse young girls and get away with it. Broadsheets were pinned to local trees and sold outside Norwich Castle on the day of his death containing a poem supposedly penned by the repenting John Self…

Sinner stop! I pray take heed
A lesson learn from this my wicked deed,
Which with shuddering frame I tell
Whilst laying in my mournful cell.

Although I doomed another not to live
And brutally took a life the Lord has pleased to give,
In this my dismal cell I humbly crave
My Saviour will a repentant sinner save.

It was in misfortunes darkening hour
Satan triumphed and o'er me gained power,
My senses gone, the fell fiend succeed
Madly did I commit this dreadful deed.

A guilty conscience accuses me,
In frightful dreams I think I see
My tortured victim writhing on the ground
Whist crimson gore pours from every wound

Again I see her with imploring eyes,
And hands outstretched pointing to the skies
She piously implores her life to spare
And cries "Of Self! Think of our Father there."

Joanna Elphick

How shall I meet My Saviour dear,
When before him in awful judgement I appear.
Let my last moments to earnest prayer be given
That our prayers Lord may pardon me in Heaven.

Justly denied all mercy by my judges here
I humbly crave a pardon there.
Kind Christians all I pray forgive the Wretch by law
Doomed not to live.

God grant these verses may a warning be
Unto all them that hear of me
Dare not to take that which you cannot give.
Think of John Self - be warned - and happy live.

Chapter 4

A Death in the Old Red Barn

Take one ne'er-do-well wealthy farmer's son, a vivacious, saucy mole-catcher's daughter, an unwanted pregnancy and a pistol - set the scene in a sleepy Suffolk village under the shadow of the now infamous Red Barn and you have the beginnings of East Anglian folklore…

The Corders were an extremely wealthy, albeit unlucky, family who resided at Corder House in Polstead. Their three hundred acre farm employed the vast majority of the village in one way or another, most of whom were also tenants on their land. Yes, in the early eighteen hundreds to be a Corder was to be influential, rich and powerful. Not that they were overly honourable folk. Both sons had an unsavoury reputation as womanisers and wastrels. William, or 'Foxey' as he was known, was a particularly unpleasant character, forging cheques, stealing pigs and generally sneaking about the county up to no good.

Further through the village lived the Martens. Mr Marten was an honest, hard-working mole catcher, Mrs Marten kept house and looked after the younger children, but it was Maria Marten, their daughter, who caught the wandering eyes of both Corder sons.

Maria Marten's Cottage

Maria was a worldly-wise beauty who had already been seduced and abandoned with an illegitimate baby by the elder son. At twenty-five she was, as the locals would say, 'no better than what she ought to be'. A second child, Thomas Henry, the result of another liaison, lived in the Martens' cottage. The infant's father had no interest in Maria after the affair had fizzled out but he was inclined to send money when he could to help provide clothes and food.

To the outside world it appeared that Corder had a blessed life with four strong, intelligent sons and a beautiful family home, but dire events were to quickly change his fortune into sorrows and taint the family name forever. A freak accident resulted in the death of Corder's eldest son, followed by the deaths of three more sons, and finally the old man himself passed away, leaving 'Foxey' William and his mother at Corder House.

Within a matter of months William had gone from the disappointing 'black sheep' of the family to the head of the household, a position he was ill-suited to. His selfish manner and loutish behaviour did not sit well with the other farmers and tenants that he was now forced to deal with. His dalliance with Maria was also becoming a major inconvenience since it had resulted in her becoming pregnant.

Corder House as it stands today

Maria, on the other hand, took the pregnancy as another 'bump' in the road. Being a wily girl she could see this latest turn of affairs as a bargaining chip to get her feet under the Corder table. With this in mind she began to badger the increasingly irate William into marriage. Although he was not completely averse to the concept, you can be sure that for every flutter of Maria's eyelashes, Mrs Corder was pouring poison into his ear; under no circumstances was such a girl to take on the good name of Corder. If she ever found out that Maria was 'in the family way' William's life would not be worth living. He needed to act quickly.

In 1827 Maria was unceremoniously bundled off to Sudbury where she secretly gave birth to their child. The event remained unknown to all but the Martens, who took Maria and the infant back as soon as she could travel. Within two weeks, the tragic child died - a fortuitous event for William that raised more than eyebrows at the subsequent trial. The cause of death was never established since nobody actually knew of the baby and it seemed logical to be equally surreptitious in its removal. Maria and William crammed the unnamed infant in an old box and buried it in a field. Just another inconvenience disposed of in their grubby, sordid lives.

Whether or not Maria felt any regret regarding her baby's end no one will ever know but it soon became apparent to her that William might just be as unsavoury as his reputation suggested. Not only was he willing to coldly discard their child, he was happy to steal from her other offspring too. Her future husband had taken a £5 pound note from the father of young Thomas Henry, promising to pass on the considerable sum to Maria.

However, it was not long before William had stifled Maria's indignation and diverted the spotlight away from his own misgivings. Rumour had it, so he claimed, that the Parrish Officers had gathered information regarding Maria's bawdy life and bastard children. They were on their way to Marten Cottage in order to prosecute her. They had but a matter of days to take action.

Murderous East Anglia

It was no surprise that it was William who came up with a plan involving Maria leaving Polstead for good. On Friday 18th May William arrived at the cottage with very bad news. A warrant had been granted for the arrest of one Maria Marten and a constable was coming to take her away. Maria was understandably terrified. How could she leave in broad daylight when she would almost certainly be spotted by her approaching would-be captor? Once again, William had the answer. Maria was to dress in men's clothes so as to be unrecognisable and was to make her way to the Red Barn where William would be waiting. The pair could then wait until dusk and leave for Ipswich where they could finally wed. It was a perfect plan.

Situated on Barnfield Hill, the now infamous Red Barn was a local landmark, so called because of the red clay-tiled roof that hung to the left of its main door. Maria pulled on the workman's trousers and shirt, kissed her family goodbye and began the muddy half mile walk up to where her lover was waiting. She was never seen again… in one piece.

In the following months Corder proceeded to weave a tapestry of lies in order to cover up the apparent disappearance of Maria. Initially he wrote to the Martens explaining that they were indeed married but they feared the reaction from his mother would not be pleasant so they intended to extend the honeymoon period until she had somewhat calmed down. Mr and Mrs Marten offered to travel up to Ipswich in order to see their daughter and deliver Thomas Henry, who missed his mother. Letters now began to arrive from the Isle of Wight, where the new Mr and Mrs Corder were living.

Ironically, William had met a young lady by the name of Mary Moore whilst on the Isle of Wight and she would indeed become his wife. 'Foxey' Corder, convinced that he had bamboozled the Martens, now travelled to London where he advertised for a wife. One young applicant was none other than the pretty girl he had met whilst on the run. Mary Moore had absolutely no idea of William's past and by late November the pair became husband and wife. Having moved to Brentford the new Mrs Corder opened a Ladies' Boarding House and settled down into married life. William, on the other hand, became increasingly rowdy at night, where his nightmares often ended in bouts of uncontrollable screaming.

But William was not the only one suffering from strange dreams. Back in Polstead, Mrs Marten complained of fearful reoccurring nightmares in which a spectral Maria pointed to the dusty floor of the Red Barn, howling up at the night sky before disappearing into the ground. Eventually a combination of bad dreams and no word from his daughter led Tom Marten to take a walk up to the old Red Barn.

On a warm April morning in 1828, Mr Marten poked his mole-catching stick into the floor of the barn. Mud, mud, soil clods... Tom was ready to leave when something made him turn about and plunge the stick into the ground one last time. The stick slid into something soft. As he pulled it out an overwhelming stench of decay filled his nostrils. The remnants of rotting flesh clung to his stick, which he threw across the room as he fled. Mr Marten had finally found his daughter.

The partially decomposing body was still intact enough to establish identification. Maria's missing tooth was also missing from the discovered jawbone and Ann, Maria's sister, was prepared to identify her hair at the inquest held at the *Cock Inn*. A green handkerchief, known to be Corder's, was tied around the mangled neck.

The investigation took off at a flying pace. The local constable, Mr Ayres, obtained an address from William's friend and, with the help of a London officer by the name of Mr Lea, tracked him down to Brentford, where he was duly arrested.

The trial was a media sensation. By mid-July all hotels in Bury St Edmunds were full, waiting for court proceedings to commence. On the 7th August 1828 the viewing gallery was heaving and the pavement outside was crowded with disappointed members of the public who could not fit into the courtroom. Ladies, unable to enter the building, hitched up their skirts and climbed onto the outside wall and railings in the hopes of a glimpse of the diabolical Corder.

William calmly pleaded 'not guilty' to a total of ten indictments of murder from a plethora of methods. The body of poor old Maria had yielded a variety of possible ends ranging from stabbing, strangulation, shooting, eye popping to piercing a dagger through the heart.

The surprising and all too titillating arrival of Maria herself, in the form of a pair of broken ribs and the decomposing heart, created a level of frenzy never seen before. Sexual philanderers, illegitimate children, pistols, intrigue and lies; what a piece of theatre!

Although William gave a rousing performance in the dock, claiming that he had heard a pistol fire and entered the barn to find his beloved on the floor, the jury were unimpressed. They returned in under forty minutes with a guilty verdict.

The judge, Baron Alexander, passed the death sentence and ordered that his body be dissected and anatomized.

"And may the Lord God Almighty, of his infinite goodness, have mercy on your soul."

Wow what a finale!

The cocky young fellow who had entered the dock was no longer to be seen. It was a weak and clearly shaken William that was led from the court. Having languished in gaol for three days, Corder finally confessed to the killing of Maria. He swore that the death had been accidental, having shot her in the eye as she was removing her disguise. He had never stabbed her in the heart. This, he claimed, must have been the result of Tom Marten's stick being pushed through the floor. Either way, Corder was set to swing on August 11th 1828.

The execution was a major event in criminal history. It was later claimed that as many as 20,000 spectators flooded the streets of Bury St Edmunds and news of his demise reached far and wide. That night, during a performance of *Macbeth* in Drury Lane, London, an actor spoke the lines, "Is execution done on Cawdor" only to be heckled by a member of the audience with "Yes! He was hung this morning at Bury."

The dissection was a gruesome affair enticing crowds in excess of 5,000 into the Shire Hall courtroom where his body was left on display. Having sliced the body open, thereby exposing the muscles, Cambridge University students were invited to witness the post-mortem.

Further phrenological studies based around the popular science of the day led the surgeons to conclude that Corder's skull displayed secretive and destructive characteristics. Whether this was retrospective brilliance or sheer coincidence, the medics appeared to have summed 'little Foxey' Corder up perfectly.

Maria's body was finally laid to rest in St Mary's Churchyard where her bones lie to this very day.

Resting place of Maria Marten

Legal Ponderings - Criminal Memorabilia

Although criminals today are not allowed to make money out of their brutal deeds and infamous standing, criminal memorabilia is much sort after. Serial killers may not sell their autographs to ghoulish groupies but should a signature make its way onto the open market it will cause far more interest than a signed photograph of Tom Cruise or a member of the Royal Family. This, of course, is not a new situation. The death of Maria Marten is a perfect example since her tragic murder and the subsequent execution of William Corder created its own industry only to be equalled by the later sensational crimes of Jack the Ripper.

Over a million Broadsides were sold detailing William's final hours along with appallingly sentimental ballads and crude woodcuts of his execution.

Corder's executioner, John Foxton, was offered the murderer's trousers as of right, whilst pieces of the rope were sold off for one guinea each. Selling the rope was a lucrative sideline for any hangman instigating the adage, 'money for old rope'.

Other gory souvenirs included locks of Maria's hair, cheap at two guineas, a section of Corder's scalp and his skeleton, which was rigged to point to a collection box situated at the entrance of the West Suffolk Hospital - a gruesome but effective way of parting visitors from their small change.

Copies of the waxy Death Mask were distributed all across the country as collectors jostled for the best memorabilia, whilst the prize for most macabre souvenir went to an account of the murder bound in Corder's tanned skin.

Polstead became an enormously popular tourist attraction. Thousands came to trample across Maria's grave, chipping away at her tombstone until eventually it was removed altogether. The Barn was pulled apart for a variety of vile gifts, possibly the worst being a collection of toothpicks made from the wooden planks lining the walls. In 1842 a bizarre fire broke out, burning the Red Barn to the floor, leaving behind a desolate landscape.

Barnfield Hill

Before the trial had even taken place plays were being performed up and down the country. Accounts of the crime were written by various notaries including Charles Dickens and James Curtis.

To date five films have been made recreating the sordid death of Maria Marten and to this day, plays such as *Maria Marten or Murder in the Red Barn* are performed to delighted audiences everywhere.

Chapter 5

When Love Goes Wrong, Nothing Goes Right

Catherine and John Foster had been sweethearts since the age of fourteen, so what on earth possessed her to coldly murder him three weeks after their wedding day? This question has plagued crime historians over a century but unfortunately, the only one who could explain swung for her crime at the tender age of seventeen.

At twelve years of age, Catherine Morley had already attracted the attention of local lad John Foster. Although she was far too young to consider marriage, John, seven years her senior, made it plain that this was his long-term plan.

At fourteen, Catherine left school and found herself in domestic service, a job she thoroughly enjoyed. She successfully worked at a variety of posts from Bulmer to Great Waldingfield until September 1846 when she was finally dismissed. Catherine was crushed. She loved the freedom that employment had given her and had been proud to send home money for her mother and siblings. John, who had continued to court her throughout

Joanna Elphick

her time in service, saw this new situation as something of a blessing. As an apprentice working at Chilton, he had money to spare and took no time in offering it to Mrs Morley if she would kindly take him in as her lodger. Catherine's mother was uncomfortable with this suggestion considering the nature of his relationship with her daughter. However, Catherine's dismissal had left a considerable hole in their finances.

It was at this point that John played his trump card. If Mrs Morley gave her blessing, the pair could be married, thereby retaining all sense of propriety and increasing the household income. It was a win win situation since it meant financial security for the family and John would finally take his childhood sweetheart for a wife.

Mrs Morley readily agreed and the pair hastily wed on 28th October 1846 at All Saints Church in Acton.

All Saints Church today

Murderous East Anglia

So far, our tale seems quite an ordinary one. Two young people meet, fall in love and end up happily married. Delightful! Unfortunately, things were about to take a rather unusual turn.

A mere three days after the quiet wedding ceremony, Catherine Foster decided to take a trip to visit her Auntie in Pakenham. It is hard to decide which is more bizarre, Catherine wishing to leave her handsome, new husband so soon after their wedding vows or John happily watching his young wife disappear for two weeks. Either way, off she went and John did not seem to mind.

On her return, things slipped into a steady pattern. John went off to work and Catherine stayed at home to cook and clean. Mrs Morley left early each morning to do washing in the village. Three weeks after their marriage Catherine took the time out to visit her mother-in-law. The two chatted of this and that until the shadows grew long. Catherine bade Old Mrs Foster farewell, apologising for her sudden departure. She had promised to make dumplings for dinner since it was John's favourite and it would take some time although she already had the ingredients. It is an icy thought that Catherine might have fully intended to poison her husband that night and was gaily discussing the details of his demise with poor John's mother.

The next few hours were reconstructed at the trial through the evidence of Catherine's nine-year-old brother, Thomas. He had come back from school and watched his sister making the dinner, as he often did. This time, he noted, Catherine made two separate dumplings. The first was kneaded and left in the boiler as usual. The second, however, was given extra care since it was to be left for John when he got home from work. His sister carefully emptied a small twist of paper into the mixture. When asked what was in the paper, Thomas replied that it was a dark powder, one that he had never seen Catherine use before. The two dumplings were boiled and John's was lovingly wrapped in cheesecloth.

Thomas and Catherine sat down to eat the first dumpling when John walked through the door, tired and hungry from a day in the fields. It was now six o'clock as the three huddled around the fire sharing stories of their day.

Part way through the meal John began to complain of sharp pains in the chest and stomach. Deciding it was probably heartburn, he left his plate and walked across the kitchen only to wretch uncontrollably. Moments later Catherine found her husband doubled up in the backyard being violently sick. By seven o'clock Mrs Morley came home to find her son-in-law screaming in pain whilst Catherine tried to cover him with blankets and clear up the dark, glutinous vomit that filled buckets and basins around the room. She took charge immediately, ordering Catherine to run over to the *Crown Inn* to buy brandy. Ironically it would be here, at the Inn, that the inquest into John's death would take place a few days later.

The Crown Inn as it stands today.

Catherine returned with the drink but by this time the situation was far worse. No sooner had the brandy been consumed, John disgorged it. Not only that, he had also begun to suffer from diarrhoea. Throughout the night the women sat by his bed, washing away the vomit and desperately trying to banish the offensive, foetid odours.

Things had not improved by morning and so at first light Catherine began the tiring journey to Long Melford to call upon the doctor there. Unfortunately for John, Dr Jones had recently dealt with a case of English Cholera and blithely assumed this to be a similar situation. Mrs Foster was briskly sent away with the typical medication of the day. Needless to say, it didn't work.

John grew weaker and weaker by the hour until eventually in the early afternoon, he died.

Dr Jones was called and quickly assessed the situation. Clearly John's case of Cholera had set in too deeply before the medication had reached him. A sad end for a God-fearing man, but nothing unusual. Just to be on the safe side, his stomach and intestines were carefully removed for further investigation.

Catherine played the broken-hearted widow beautifully but her foul play was soon to be highlighted by a different kind of fowl. The following day a number of chickens went missing from the neighbour's field only to be found dead in Mrs Morley's backyard. On closer inspection it became clear that they had been eating the remains of John Foster's meal.

A coroner's inquest took place at the *Crown* and Dr Jones was requested to take the organs to Bury St Edmunds to be analysed. John's body was exhumed for further examination. It did not take them long to discover considerable quantities of arsenic. The cottage was searched but no further trace of the poison was ever found. The chickens, on the other hand, had died of arsenic poisoning. Young Thomas's description of the extra ingredient in John's dumpling was more than enough to charge Catherine with murder.

Her guilt seemed obvious but what was the motive? Nobody had ever heard Catherine and John arguing and their recent marriage had appeared to be a joyous occasion. Some thought that she missed her life in domestic service. Others claimed that she was little more than a simpleton, a 'moron' who was not prepared for marital life. Who could say? Whatever the reason, she had dealt with her problems in a cold and calculated fashion and now she would pay the price.

The trial took place at Bury St Edmunds in late March where it took the jury fifteen minutes to return a verdict of guilty. Her execution took place on Saturday 17th April 1847 before an estimated crowd of 10,000. She was barely seventeen years old.

Legal Ponderings -Capital Punishment

By 1847 many people were calling for the abolition of the death penalty. A number of petitions were circulated at the time of Catherine's trial begging for clemency but to no avail. However, due to the public outpouring, Mrs Foster was the last woman to be publicly executed in Suffolk. From this point on, women were at least afforded some privacy in their final hour.

People are often shocked at the time scale of capital punishment in the UK. A time line puts the history of executions in this country into some context and shows the gradual change in public opinion.

- 1808: Samuel Romilly introduced reforms to abolish capital punishment for a number of offences under the 'Bloody Code'

- 1832-34: Four more offences were removed from the 'Bloody Code' including 'letter stealing' and 'sacrilege'

- 1843: Gibbeting was abolished

- 1861: Capital crimes were reduced to four - murder, treason, arson in a Royal dockyard and piracy with violence

- 1868: Public executions were abolished

- 1870: Execution by 'hung, drawn and quartered' abolished

- 1908: People under sixteen could no longer be hanged

- 1922: Infanticide was no longer a capital offence

- 1931: Pregnant women could no longer be hanged

- 1955: Ruth Ellis was the last woman hanged in the UK

- 1957: The Homicide Act 1957 restricted the use of capital punishment

- 1964: Peter Anthony Allen & Gwynne Owen Evans were the last men hanged in the UK

- 1969: Capital punishment for murder was finally abolished

- 1998: High treason and piracy with violence were no longer capital crimes

- 1999: Home Secretary signed the Sixth protocol of the European Human Rights in Strasbourg, formally abolishing the death penalty in the UK

Chapter 6

In The Blood

It has often been said that certain families carry 'bad blood', an ominous statement if ever there was one. One hears the cry 'like father like son' quite regularly but what of 'like father like daughter'? Whilst researching the tragic end of John Foster, a strange piece of information was unearthed...

In 1838, one William Robert Morley was taken into custody, accused of murder. He had been found lying face down in the road in an intoxicated state claiming that he had been robbed of his pension, seven sovereigns.

He had previously been witnessed leaving Lavenham with another fellow by the name of William Kilpatrick who had also just collected his pension. The two had wandered off together in the direction of Sudbury near where Morley lived. At some point there had clearly been a robbery. Kilpatrick was found swinging from a signpost. His body was still warm.

Morley accused the deceased of the crime, stating that he had stolen his money, beat him sorely and then, in a fit of remorse, hanged himself.

An inquest was held and, understandably, great suspicion fell upon Morley; unfortunately there was little evidence to disprove his ludicrous tale. Nobody thought to check either man's pockets to see who actually had the coins in question. A supposedly shaken William Morley was released but the rumours that he had hanged a man for his pension lingered.

By 1841 William Robert Morley had fathered twelve children, one of whom, Catherine, would hang from the long drop at Bury St Edmunds some six years later. Like father like daughter? Most likely indeed.

Chapter 7

The Bootlace Beach Murder

This magnificent Victorian melodrama is filled with romance, violence and mystery. John Herbert Bennett was executed for the murder of his estranged wife, Mary Jane, but did they catch the right man?

As the sun sinks into the water and the holidaymakers have left the beach, the vast, empty sand dunes at South Beach, Great Yarmouth become a lonely, windswept and desolate place. It was during such a time in the early hours of Sunday 23rd September 1900 that a young boy of fifteen stumbled across the dead body of a woman. She had been strangled by an old bootlace wrapped tightly around her neck. Who this woman was or how she came to be unceremoniously dumped amongst the sand dunes nobody knew. She had no identifying belongings about her person and nobody recognised her. However, as time went on details would emerge of an unsavoury pair of small time crooks living off their ill-gotten gains until asphyxiation, one way or another, took both their lives.

Joanna Elphick

The sordid tale began some four years earlier when nineteen-year-old Mary Jane Clarke offered musical lessons to a boy three years her junior. John Herbert Bennett quickly became enamoured and by 1897, they were married. What followed was a life of double-dealings and criminal pastimes. Both parties were more than happy to dupe the unwary. Between them they made quite an impressive criminal career. In 1898 Mary Jane gave birth to a baby daughter, Ruby, and by 1900, the family had moved to Westgate-on-Sea where they bought a Grocery Shop. Various scams followed, culminating in a suspicious fire that wiped out the building and all its contents. With the insurance money they moved to a bigger shop and started all over again, leaving a stream of angry creditors and tradesmen in their wake.

The family was not a happy one; criminal highs were frequently punctuated with furious fights and sulking. John was obviously seeing other women, leaving a miserable Mary Jane and Ruby to fend for themselves. Eventually his master's voice shrieked for the last time. Mid-June the door slammed one final time and Bennett was gone.

As a free man, John cheered up considerably, meeting a delightfully innocent maid by the name of Alice Meadows. The pair stepped out and when Bennett proposed to the young girl, she gladly accepted. To all intents John was indeed a single man but the law, of course, would take a rather dim view of the situation. Bennett was still legally shackled to Mary Jane, a woman who needed his money for Ruby and, more importantly, had very intimate details of his shady past. This particularly squawky problem needed eradicating as soon as possible.

Mary Jane, meanwhile, had taken Ruby to Great Yarmouth where she rented a room at Mrs Rudrum's boarding house. For unknown reasons she had changed her name to Mrs Hood and in conspiratorial tones, explained to the bemused landlady that she was here to meet a lover in secret. She showed Mrs Rudrum a letter telling Mary Jane to 'meet at the Big Clock at nine o'clock'. How thrilling! Mrs Hood had dressed beautifully. The landlady was particularly impressed with the silver watch hanging around her neck on a gold chain. Various people saw an elegant woman walking through the town that night, unaware that this would be the last time she would ever be seen alive again.

When Mrs Hood failed to return the next day, leaving a distraught Ruby behind, Mrs Rudrum called in the police. It did not take them long to put the unknown woman found strangled on the dunes with the missing lodger but it soon became clear that the name 'Hood' was an alias. Hopes of establishing her true identity quickly died out and, as a result, it was a coffin marked 'unknown' that was buried in the local churchyard.

One piece of evidence continued to nag at the police: a ticket marked 599. Further inquiries confirmed that this was a laundry ticket and the water marking suggested it had originated from Bexleyheath. The other half of the stub belonged to a Mrs Bennett - another dead end, or was it? The laundry staff enquired after Mrs Bennett and her little girl who appeared to have disappeared. It was too much of a coincidence. It did not take the police officers long to join the dots together and track down Mr Bennett, whose behaviour was highly suspicious.

During this time John Herbert Bennett had lied to his beloved Alice, telling her that he needed to take time to look after his sick Grandfather in Gravesend. Alice had wished him well and returned home. Bennett had immediately changed trains, taking a trip to Great Yarmouth. On his return he announced to Alice that his Grandfather had died and he wanted to find happiness with her as soon as possible. They should speed up the marriage plans and move away. Alice was overjoyed and began preparations. In the meantime, John showered his beautiful fiancée with jewellery and clothes, all belonging to his late wife.

As the police searched Bennett's bedroom one article stood out above all others: a pretty silver watch on a long gold chain. On the face of it the evidence seemed overwhelming. John Herbert Bennett was arrested and charged with the wilful murder of his wife.

Four day committal proceedings in Great Yarmouth were followed by a scandalous trial at the Old Bailey, London on 25th February 1901. The evidence was entirely circumstantial. Even the seemingly damning jewellery could not be unequivocally identified. Motive came in the form of little Alice Meadows, the only truly innocent party in the tale that unfolded before the jury. Defence Counsel produced a previous landlady who was prepared to testify that Mrs Bennett had owned two gold chains, not one. Another witness by the unlikely name of Shalto Douglas claimed to have taken a beer with Bennett in a London pub during the evening of the murder.

Like a furiously played tennis match each side viciously attempted to undermine the other with spurious remarks and snide, contemptuous comments. Only the judge, Lord Chief Justice Alverstone, remained calm and objective.

The jury were ushered out only to return half an hour later to deliver a verdict of guilty.

The crowd outside the Old Bailey cheered wildly. Newspapers sold out in record time and, back in Norwich, traffic was diverted to accommodate the crowds waiting for extra copies to be delivered.

Bennett never changed his plea of innocence. He refused to produce a confession, claiming that to do so would be a lie before God. On 21st March 1901, John Herbert Bennett the small time crook was executed for the murder of his partner in crime and matrimony.

His defence continued to beg for leniency being completely convinced of his client's innocence. A grave injustice, he claimed, had occurred.

On a warm July morning in 1912, some eleven years after Bennett had swung for his supposed crime, a young lady by the name of Dora May Gray went missing. Her body was eventually found slumped over as if fast asleep on the sand dunes at Great Yarmouth. She had been strangled by a bootlace.

You can almost hear the Prosecution counsel's words from the trial echoing off the dunes. "The evidence may well be circumstantial members of the jury, but a wise man should never believe in coincidence for there is no such thing."

I wonder…

Joanna Elphick

Yarmouth Dunes

Chapter 8

Battered For the Last Time

The sleepy Norfolk village of Potter Heigham seems an unlikely location for a revolutionary protest but it was in this rural spot, less than ten miles from the bustling port of Great Yarmouth, that an early feminine battle was won. Unfortunately, it would be another one hundred years before the legal world truly caught up with the local people's hearts.

On a particularly frosty night in 1905, just three days after Christmas, the neighbours of Mrs Rosa Kowan were woken by the hysterical screams of "fire!" A couple of men broke down the wooden door and quickly carried the terrified woman out into the street. The flames had travelled across the parlour and were now licking the bottom of the stairs. Against Mrs Kowan's advice, one brave gentleman leapt up the steps to reach James, her husband, who, she said, had fallen asleep and could not be roused. The neighbour fought his way across the landing and entered the bedroom, only to be met with a scene of utter horror. James had clearly been

Joanna Elphick

bludgeoned to death and was lying in a pool of his own congealing blood.

Eventually the fire was brought under control and the mangled corpse of Mr Kowan was removed from the house. A shaken Rosa was quietly led away by the police and taken into custody. Fascinated onlookers watched with horrified glee as a bloody hatchet was removed from the coalhouse and a hammer covered in gore and human hair was solemnly bagged and taken away by a pale-faced police officer.

The initial trial was a farcical affair based upon circumstantial evidence, most of which was decidedly charred. Mrs Kowan pleaded 'not guilty' leaving the jury to reconcile a quiet, diminutive woman and a chopped-up cadaver. Ultimately, they agreed to disagree, leaving Mrs Kowan to face a second trial.

On 16th January, 1906 a shrunken, white-faced defendant returned to court but this time the trial took a slightly different turn. A variety of neighbours took the stand, telling tales of extraordinary cruelty and violence. Mrs Kowan had spent her entire married life in the shadow of her abusive husband. This delicate woman had often been seen with blackened eyes, a bandaged arm and cuts about the face. Neighbours told of James' booming voice disturbing their children late into the night and the sound of smashing pottery, glass and even furniture could be heard. Mrs Kowan, they claimed, was a victim, not a murderess.

The jury members were in a dilemma. The defendant was clearly guilty and should therefore hang for her crimes, but where was the justice in that? Hours ticked by but a unanimous verdict was not forthcoming. Eventually, the

Judge stepped in; if they could not come to an agreement then a third trial should be brought. The viewing gallery was in an uproar. How could they prolong this poor woman's agony any further?

Support for her release was rapidly growing but the legal system was not equipped to deal with this new way of thinking. The courts needed to avoid any further unwanted publicity and it was decided that Mrs Kowan should be quietly removed. A warrant for her release was surreptitiously given in the hopes that she, and the problem would disappear. However, this monumental victory for abused women everywhere was not going to occur without celebration.

As Mrs Kowan was silently led out of the side door of the court the street outside erupted in cheers. Well-wishers threw flowers as the car carrying their newfound heroine drove slowly past.

What happened to Mrs Kowan is not known. She was taken back to her home where she was allowed to pack one suitcase before being put on a train to start a new life. One hopes that she left the cruelty and humiliation of her former life to find happiness far, far away from Potter Heigham.

Legal Ponderings - Provocation and Loss of Control

Today, Mrs Kowan would be said to have suffered from Battered Wife Syndrome, a concept propounded by the eminent QC Helena Kennedy.

The situation where a woman kills her husband because of years of abuse is a legal minefield. She could not claim the partial defence to murder of Provocation under s.3 of the Homicide Act 1957 since she would, almost certainly, have had time to 'cool off' after the last abusive bout before she struck. This opportunity for the perpetrator of the crime to calm down after the provoking act of the victim, negated the defence entirely and, of course, very few women have ever attacked their violent partners during a beating.

Until the courts were prepared to accept Battered Wife Syndrome as a psychiatric condition, these women could not use the defence of Diminished Responsibility under s.2 of the Homicide Act since they were said to have 'no inherent condition, causing an abnormality of the mind'. Without the acceptance from the court that a continuous fear of physical, sexual or psychological abuse caused such a condition, any woman who ended her pain with the death of the 'problem' was called a murderer and given a mandatory life sentence.

Women such as Thornton and Duffy highlighted the injustice but it was not until the case of R v Ahluwalia in 1992 that the defence of Diminished Responsibility by Battered Wife Syndrome was successful, thereby allowing such women the justice that had been denied them for so many years.

In 2009 The Coroners and Justice Act abolished the defence of Provocation and, in its place, created the defence of Loss of Control. This new defence can be used by battered wives without having to acknowledge any mental disturbance. Rather, they can claim that, through fear, they lost control of themselves and struck out at the victim. There is no longer a need to show a lack of any time delay, thereby avoiding the issue of an abused wife lashing out whilst the husband slept.

How interesting to think that it all began one hundred years ago by a quiet, unassuming lady in a sleepy, East Anglian village.

Chapter 9

The Stanfield Hall Slayings

As with many a woeful tale, this particular story begins with a desperate situation of humiliating financial trouble and the inevitable bitter seeds of resentment…

In 1837 Mr Isaac Jermy, an influential and popular member of the community being both Chairman at Quarter Sessions and Recorder at Norwich, inherited the magnificent Stanfield Hall Estate from his deceased father. The property windfall, although gratefully received, was not without its problems. Firstly the inheritance itself was in question. Other members of the Jermy family felt somewhat aggrieved at the legacy; particularly Jermy's cousin, John Larner, who doubted the legality of the benefaction and ultimately stormed the Hall in an unsuccessful bid to take it from him.

Secondly, not all of the estate tenants were overly forthcoming in the delivery of their rent. The worst of these was a principal tenant by the name of James Blomfield Rush, who resided at the impressive Potash Farm whilst also maintaining two further properties on the estate. Tension between landlord and tenant came to a head when Jermy decided to increase the rent on two of the dwellings leased to Rush.

With much wrangling and begging on James' part, Jermy agreed to sell Potash Farm to him and even offered a ten year mortgage in which to do it. Rush snapped up the offer with little or no thought for the future and in doing so tied himself financially to Jermy and buried himself further in debt.

The unexpected death of Mrs Blomfield Rush left James a single father of nine children and a man in considerable financial difficulties. He owed mortgage payments on Potash Farm, rents on two further properties and a humiliating court payment for breach of promise to a young girl he had agreed to marry many years earlier. Having taken her innocence, the unprincipled Rush had fled the scene leaving behind a ruined girl and a furious father. The law had eventually caught up with him but he had successfully kept his sordid past hidden from his late wife, associates and creditors.

James Blomfield Rush clearly needed a plan. Firstly, he needed someone to help look after the children. In 1846 he employed a governess, one Emily Sandford. The young girl was carefully ensconced in one of the rented properties, Stanfield Hall Farm, and immediately took to the upbringing of the motherless children. Meanwhile Rush began grooming the rather innocent and somewhat green governess for various other roles. Initially, Rush viewed Emily as a rather convenient sexual plaything. After all, she was pretty, virtuous and above all else, within easy reach. The gullible Ms Sandford looked upon Rush with a mixture of awe and desirability. To the untrained eye he appeared quite a catch and It didn't take too much persuading from the silver-tongued Rush for her to 'let her guard down' somewhat. After all, he fully intended to marry her when the time was right and in the interim, she could remain undetected as the family governess.

Of course, having relinquished her virtue, Emily was somewhat at the mercy of her unethical lover. She could not afford to irritate him in any way since she was likely to lose far more than her job should he tire of her charms. As time slipped by Rush began to embroil the dutiful girl in his wicked schemes.

For decency's sake, the young Ms Sandford was moved to Mylne Street, Pentonville, where James could meet with her under the guise of a much loved 'uncle', thereby keeping their guilty tryst hidden from view. From Rush's position it was also a useful meeting place where iniquitous transactions could transpire. Larner and other disgruntled members of the Jermy family were invited to the townhouse to make plans for the usurpation of poor Isaac Jermy. Blomfield Rush was more than happy to help remove their 'little problem' if, in return, they rearranged his financial ties to the estate. Documents were quickly drawn up promising extended leases and mortgages as soon as Larner was firmly installed at Stanfield Hall. An unwitting Ms Sandford acted as a witness, signing any and all papers put before her.

Unfortunately her involvement did not end there. Having waved their co-conspirators off James instructed Emily to draw up a second, far more worrying document. This paper suggested that Isaac Jermy would give up the mortgage in return for unequivocal support from Rush regarding possession of the Stanfield Hall Estates. All Emily had to do was sign it as a witness; James would see that Isaac would add his signature on his return to Norfolk. The young governess was understandably concerned by this sudden change of tack but hoped that her mysterious lover knew what he was doing. After all, he was a good and honourable man deserving of her trust. Emily signed the documents and hoped for the best.

This latest forged contract was, of course, worthless unless Isaac Jermy should drop dead before 28th November when the mortgage on Potash Farm would come to an end and all financial promises were to be met. Jermy, it has to be said, was looking irritatingly well and any sudden death throes looked highly unlikely. No, Jermy had to die before the end of November if Rush was to remain at Potash Farm.

Isaac Jermy was a genteel man of habit. Each evening, having finished supper, the Recorder of Norwich took a brief stroll, taking in the air before retiring to the drawing room for a lively chat or game of cards with his family, and 28th November was no exception. The weather on that fateful night was not overly conducive to a potter round the grounds. The wind was up, rattling the overgrown bushes and sending the autumn leaves flying in all directions. The clouds were gathering in the evening sky, suggesting more than a hint of rain but Isaac Jermy was a hardy soul so out he stepped through the porch doors and into the garden.

Mr Jermy had barely let go of the door handle when a shadowy figure slipped out from the bushes and lumbered towards him dressed quite bizarrely in a woman's frock and swirling cloak. His face, for it was undeniably a man's gait, was covered by a scarf and large hat. Within moments of his arrival, the stranger produced two pistols from beneath his voluminous attire. A shot was fired and Isaac Jermy sank to the ground. The bullet had shattered his ribs and pierced his heart, leaving him dead.

Joanna Elphick

At this point a living nightmare descended upon Stanfield Hall as the menacing intruder stalked through the family home reeking vengeance and misguided retribution. On hearing the first shot both the Butler and young Mr Jermy ran out into the hall to see what had occurred. The monstrous figure turned and fired a second time, striking Jermy Junior at point-blank range. His death was almost as sudden as his father's a few moments previously.

By now the entire household had been alerted as to the danger and everybody reacted accordingly. Martha Read, the cook, had rushed up from the kitchens and seeing the ghastly sight of young Mr Jermy lying on the floor and Mrs Sophie Jermy desperately trying to rouse her husband, grabbed the hand of their daughter, fourteen year old Isabella and pulled her into the shadows as the intruder stormed out of the Lobby and into the dining room. As soon as he had passed, Martha dragged the terrified child back to the kitchens where they escaped through the servants' entrance into the night.

Eliza, the maid, bravely tried to comfort her mistress who had by now realised her husband was dead. The pair of distraught young women had left the body and were in the process of finding somewhere to hide when the killer returned. Two more shots were fired; one hit Mrs Sophie Jermy in the arm as she attempted to shield them from his fury, the other caught Eliza in the leg, shattering the bone. With this final act of cruel vengeance, the hideous figure pulled his cloak about him and disappeared out through the porch door, leaving a behind a handwritten note that fluttered to the ground in his wake.

By this time the butler had reached a neighbouring farm and called for help. Norwich police were alerted and the local Magistrate from Wymondham arrived to oversee the proceedings. One thing was perfectly clear to those at the scene. Throughout this ghastly, traumatic event everybody was of exactly the same opinion - the shadowy killer was definitely James Blomfield Rush. The grotesque disguise and muffled voice appeared to have had no effect since Rush had been easily identified by both servants and family members alike. But what of the note left by the killer...

There are seven of us here, three of us outside, and four inside the hall, all armed as you see us two. If any of you servants offer to leave the premises or to follow, you will be shot dead. Therefore, all of you keep in the servants' hall, and you nor anyone else will take any harm, for we only come to take of the Stansfield Hall property.

It was signed, Thomas Jermy, the Owner.

The survivors were not swayed by the writing, it was merely a diversion; Blomfield Rush was the killer.

On their arrival from Norwich, a number of policemen were deployed immediately to Potash Farm where Rush was duly arrested and taken to Wymondham Bridewell leaving a shaken Emily Sandford behind. After an inquest at The King's Head, Rush was transferred to Norwich Castle whilst awaiting his trial.

On 29th March 1849, the six day trial of James Blomfield Rush began. It was to be a sorry, sordid life that unfolded before the jury's eyes, full of subterfuge, salacious behaviour and general cruelty. Here before them stood a man of low morals and few scruples. And yet throughout the entire trial, Rush doggedly attempted to maintain his paper-thin image as a devout family man. It was a pitiful performance that frequently fell, allowing a glimpse of the real monster beneath.

Base as the contents were, the trial, heard before Mr Baron Rolfe, was not without great excitement and one or two theatricals. The arrival of young Eliza Chestney, the brave housemaid, was of particular note since she was brought into court reclining on a couch made for the purpose of transporting her during her convalescence. The delicate creature displayed steely resolve during her examination, claiming, "*I saw the man who shot me; his head was apparently flat on the top; his hair set out, or bushy on his head; he had wide shoulders. I believed at the time that the man I saw was Rush. I had no doubt in my mind about it. I still think and believe it to be Rush.*"

The spectators gallery went wild, Eliza went pink and Rush went green. Similar gasps were heard from both the jury and onlookers at the sight of the widow, Mrs Sophie Jermy, sporting a stump where her arm had once been. Oh yes, it was a dramatic trial indeed! However, it was perhaps the examination of Emily Sandford that piqued most interest. The pathetic figure of the duped mistress caused a mixture of distaste, contempt but ultimately sympathy from the court as she took the stand. She had remained loyal throughout the months up to the trial but as the true events began to unfold her devotion wavered. She was not, after all, a bad girl; her greatest fault was her gullibility and this was borne of an innocent disposition and naturally trusting nature.

Rush had foolishly decided to conduct his own defence, much to the glee of the prosecution. As Emily desperately tried to appease her lover whilst maintaining some semblance of truth, Rush became more and more irritated by her avoidance tactics. It did not take him long to realise that she had no intention of committing perjury and his questions soon turned to outright bullying. All at once the jury saw the true nature of this degrading relationship and it was at this point the defendant's case was lost. Further damning evidence from the arresting officers, who discovered a pair of recently fired pistols and muddy boots in Rush's bedroom, reassured the collective mind of the jury.

As the final day came to a close, a weary jury retired to deliberate the facts. They did not take long. Six minutes later they returned with a unanimous verdict of Guilty. Mr Baron Rolfe then proceeded to pass the death sentence. Contempt for the prisoner was no longer disguised:

In your case there is everything that could add a deeper dye to guilt the most horrible. You commenced a system of fraud by endeavouring to cheat your landlord, and you followed it up by making the unfortunate girl, whom you had seduced, a tool whereby you should commit forgery, and you terminated your guilty career by the murder of the son and grandson of your former benefactor. In your case may be seen the avenging hand of God. For had you redeemed your pledge by making that unfortunate girl your wife she could not have been a witness against you, and the evidence of your guilt would not have been conclusive.

A cold and unmoved Rush was then led away. Back at the castle, Rush continued to profess his innocence. Both warden and chaplain begged him to confess and purge his soul but their words were to no avail.

On Saturday 21st April 1849, James Blomfield Rush quietly walked to the scaffold that had been duly erected across the centre of the bridge, spanning the dry moat of Norwich castle. Spectators flocked from all about the country to see this heinous criminal swing. In fact, Rush had pulled in a crowd of over fifteen thousand. Inns and local public houses were fit to burst and all roads were blocked in or out of the City. Chimneys coughed up black smoke as hungry onlookers clamoured for food. Some had travelled a good way to witness the hanging and all wished to enjoy the festivities with food and drink.

To the very end Rush remained an arrogant, egotistical tyrant, snapping at those around him and even daring to give advice to Calcraft, the famed executioner, shrieking, "For God sake, give me rope enough."

As the clock struck the hour of twelve, the bolt was removed and the prisoner fell through the trap door to a cacophony of raucous applause. Eight hours later, having taken a cast of his head for phrenological purposes, his body was buried in a deep grave in the prison grounds. The bullying, coldly calculating murderer James Blomfield Rush was dead, but his wicked deeds lingered in the hearts of East Anglians everywhere through songs, broadsheets and dire poems such as this one, recorded on the day of his execution:

Come listen while I tell
The awful crimes of Rush,
The awful crimes of Rush,
Who dies on the gallows today.

He murdered poor Mr Jermy,
Who never did him harm.
But gave him money to spend,
And kept him out of want.

The fellow went at night
To the quiet Stanfield Hall,
And there with murderous weapons he did kill
Two unoffending men.

Two innocent women there,
Who never did him harm,
He shot at and dreadfully wounded,
The base and cruel man.

Take warning all of you,
That passion's iron sway
May never tempt you to commit
Such great and cruel sin.

Difficult as it is to believe, this particular literary disaster was considered one of the better offerings of the day, and almost certainly the most popular and most frequently recited. One can only imagine the tone of the remaining ballads.

Stanfield Hall today

Legal Ponderings - Phrenology

The head of James Blomfield Rush was of great interest to budding phrenologists and a number of casts were taken and distributed to pseudo-scientific groups across the country.

It was the Austrian physician Franz Joseph Gall who first developed the theory of Phrenology, coming from *phrenos*, 'the mind' and *logos*, 'to study'. It was initially hailed as the 'only true science of mind' but its tenets were later openly ridiculed and by the mid-nineteenth century it was completely discredited.

However, for a brief period in time, the phrenological science of character divining was enormously popular and American 'Phrenological Fowlers', china busts that mapped out vital areas of the head, could be found in every well-read Victorian gentleman's study.

The theory was basically a form of character analysis based on the bumps protruding from the scalp. Callipers were used to measure the length and elevation of a variety of raised areas and these were compared to a carefully designed model. Character, temperament and even humour could be identified with practice; it was all terribly good fun.

Of course, it did not take Phrenologists long to realise the true, profitable potential of such information. To begin with employers paid for phrenological character references. A reading that suggested a loyal and hard-working temperament opened doors and ensured secured employment. Lovelorn individuals could pay for the privilege of a perfect partner match, guaranteeing a lifetime of commitment and passion.

Of course, Blomfield's head was of little interest to single women or prospective employers. It was the criminal reformers who saw the usefulness in this new and exciting science. If wicked traits could be identified then perhaps criminals could be spotted before the crime had occurred. A multitude of guilty scalps, including Rush, Corder and many others mentioned in this book, were feverishly studied in the hopes of identifying criminal appearances.

Wax casts were sent far and wide across the country and many can still be seen in museums and Bridewells.

Unfortunately the future of Phrenology was not to last. In 1808 the Institute of France declared that there was little science involved and ultimately, was not to be relied upon. Interestingly enough, the final blow for Phrenology came from Napoleon Bonaparte, who viciously shredded its reputation after one brave soul suggested his skull lacked a variety of brave and noble qualities that he had previously assumed!

Joanna Elphick

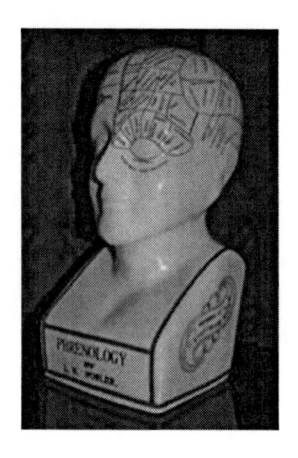

A typical Phrenological Fowler

Chapter 10

A Duel to the Death on Cawston Heath

On 21st August 1698, the last duel to be fought in Norfolk came to its bloody climax on the windswept landscape of Cawston Heath. It was a vicious fight, fuelled by resentment and an irrational hatred that could only end in death.

Sir Henry Hobart, the Fourth Baronet of Blickling Hall, had been knighted by Charles II as a boy and rapidly grew into an impatient, pompous Member of Parliament.

Blickling Hall

He acted for the Whig Party, successfully representing Kings Lynn until a series of slanderous rumours suggesting that whilst serving in Ireland he had been a coward during the Battle of the Boyne undermined public confidence and he found himself without a seat.

Shock and disbelief soon gave way to a seething rage that was only confounded by a humiliating, ever-deepening financial crisis. His political ambitions had quickly eaten away at his wealth, leaving him to fend off creditors and put pressure on his tenants.

Hobbart had reached boiling point and therefore needed somewhere to release his fury. A passing comment that a local Tory had started the vicious rumours of his cowardice was all he needed. Every ounce of pent-up rage and frustration was immediately turned upon an unsuspecting lawyer living quietly at Great Witchingham Hall.

Great Witchingham Hall

Sir Oliver Le Neve was everything Hobbart wasn't; a jolly, well-respected squire and extremely wealthy tradesman descended from an ancient family. Whilst Sir Henry prided himself on his superb swordsmanship, Sir Oliver spent any spare time drinking with friends or quietly fishing.

When pressed, Le Neve categorically refuted the allegations. He had no interest in Hobbart or his conduct on the battlefield and as such, considered that the problem had been successfully resolved. It had not. Hobbart wanted blood - public violent correction for his deep humiliation.

A duel to the death was called for but Le Neve balked at the idea. He was a thirty-six year old JP and a tradesman with a beautiful young family. Sir Henry was a renowned hothead and a fine swordsman. Taking him on would be suicide and Sir Oliver had far too much to live for. A letter was speedily written and sent to Hobbart, calling for a calm solution. The letter was read and dismissed within a heartbeat.

The next few weeks were deeply distressing for Le Neve. Initially his time was spent setting his affairs in order, overseeing his wife's financial security and finalising all aspects of his will. Having kissed his wife and children goodbye, he left Great Witchingham Hall and headed towards an almost certain death.

A thick mist shrouded the scrubland as the two men met and bowed. As each took the proper stance, a young serving girl hiding in the bushes watched the duel unfold with a mixture of awe and foreboding. Her account of the duel would later prove to be pivotal at the trial.

Hobart lunged and parried from the start, attacking Le Neve with such ferocity that within minutes his arm had been pierced and he began to bleed profusely. Although weakened, all was not lost for Oliver Le Neve. Nature had given him an unexpected advantage; he was left-handed. A desperate stab took Hobart by surprise since he had not envisaged such a return from the left. As the blade sliced through his waistcoat and opened his stomach, Sir Henry Hobart fell to his knees, clutching his gaping wound and shrieking with a combination of fear and fury. The duel was over but the drama had only just begun.

Without seconds to oversee the duel, the event that had just transpired was considered to be illegal and, unbeknownst to both men, the proceedings had been witnessed in full. Hobart quickly returned to Blickling Hall where he was lovingly tended to by his wife. Unfortunately her ministrations were not overly effective and he died in agony the following day. Lady Hobart was utterly distraught, calling for the immediate apprehension of her husband's murderer.

Oliver Le Neve barely had time to dress his wounds and send word to his wife before escaping to foreign shores. With a hefty price upon his head, Le Neve fled to Holland where he remained for two years. A trial took place in his absence at Thetford Assizes and, not surprisingly, he was found guilty. Now considered to be an outlaw, he survived through the secret gifts of money bundles and food parcels sent by his wife and loyal friends. Le Neve was free but desperately lonely. He missed his family most keenly and, having remained in hiding for over twenty four months, he decided to return home. Within this time Lady Hobart had grown utterly bored of the trial. She had moved on with her life and no longer clamoured for revenge. A second marriage sealed her disinterest and it appeared that Oliver's life could finally be restored. Life as a fugitive had taken its toll and although he initially took on a secret identity, he quickly decided to give himself up.

A new trial was begun but allegiance had shifted and, since Lady Hobart had no interest in the proceedings, the Grand Jury acquitted him. A tired and exhausted Oliver Le Neve could finally return to his family. He was no longer a hunted man, wanted for a murder he had begged to play no part in, but bad luck and melancholy trailed in his wake.

In 1703, his second wife, Jane Knyvet, passed away. Some four years later he married for a third time but the poor girl died within three months of her wedding day. A short while later, tragedy struck once more as Le Neve's son died suddenly. At this point the once jolly, happy-go-lucky tradesman appeared to lose interest in life altogether and in 1711, at the age of forty-nine, he fell asleep never to wake. Memories of the last duel in Norfolk could finally be laid to rest.

Joanna Elphick

A commemorative stone was erected to mark the site of the last duel in Norfolk but this was eventually moved to a tiny plot alongside the B1149 close to the Cawston petrol station.

Legal Ponderings - Duelling

The fine art of Duelling reached Great Britain at the tail end of the sixteenth Century thanks to a number of popular publications including the *Code Duello* and *Libro del Cortegiano* from Renaissance Italy. British aristocrats were quick to adopt the heated 'Laws of Honour', fighting to protect a besmirched reputation or sullied name.

However, not everyone was impressed by such unbridled displays of passionate angst. James I publicly castigated the practice, eventually leading to the issue of an edict in 1614 forbidding its continuance. However, Royal disdain did little to dissuade the nobility from 'demanding satisfaction' when necessary.

The duel evolved and mutated over time, eventually forgoing the sword for pistols. By the late 1700s military officers, gentlemen of society, doctors, the legal profession and even some clergymen were settling their differences with a 'polite exchange of bullets'. A number of Prime Ministers engaged in duels, including William Pitt the Younger in 1798 and the Duke of Wellington in 1829. A young actor by the name of Gabriel Spencer was killed by playwright Ben Johnson in 1598 and even the 'Grand Old Duke of York', HRH

Joanna Elphick

The Duke of York, was struck by a bullet in 1798 when he duelled with Lieutenant-Colonel Charles Lennox.

Although swords and later pistols were the common choice of weapon, some duellists substituted the usual for the bizarre: poisoned sausages, hammers, balls, even pig poo, but ultimately the anti-duellists had their way and the last duel was played out in 1852.

Chapter 11

Who Should Hang for the Death of Mrs Candler?

When Harriet Candler was found beaten to death in her own shop, a number of suspects were brought forward but, ironically, only the one who tried to save his neck would actually hang for the crime...

In the early hours of Tuesday 19th November 1844, two policemen were patrolling the shop fronts of Great Yarmouth. An unprecedented crime wave was sweeping the country; theft, violent assaults and robbery were all on the rise. A visible police presence was called for and, as a result, constables flooded the streets on a nightly basis.

As the officers passed 79 Howard Street South something made them check the front door - it was unlocked. Suspicious, they decided to enter the shop and take a look around. Carrying their lamps aloft, the two men proceeded to check the room. Everything appeared to be in order but as they turned to leave the building the lamp light lit the back of the shop counter. There, crumpled on the floor like a life-sized ragdoll, lay a woman. Her throat had been sliced open, leaving a gaping wound. She had been beaten about the head, resulting in five large injuries about the eyes, scalp and nose. In short, the shopkeeper had been violently beaten to death. A hastily dropped knife lay by her side.

Evidence was gathered and further police back-up was called for. The owner of the property, a solicitor by the name of William Catchpole, was summoned to the station where he gave a solid alibi. He had been out with friends during the night of the murder and had not returned to the house until the early hours of the morning. He had bumped into another tenant of the building on his way up to bed but, other than that, nothing untoward or unusual had occurred. A coroner soon confirmed that the deceased had already been murdered by this time. Samuel Yarham agreed with the timings, claiming that he had spent the entire evening in his room. He had heard nothing.

Mrs Candler was a popular and helpful shopkeeper. Why would anyone want to savagely attack her? The police soon discovered that the forty-six year old woman had recently come into a substantial sum of cash and this information was widely known. When a Mrs Dick arrived at the station with three bags containing money and tied with a tag inscribed 'Harriet Candler' they soon established a motive -robbery.

The police were suspicious of the lodger, Yarham. How was it possible that a violent attack ending in murder could have occurred without him hearing any noise, particularly since the walls were paper-thin? Their scepticism increased tenfold on the arrival of a young constable who claimed he had witnessed Samuel Yarham walking away from the shop in the very early hours of the morning. Meanwhile other witnesses came forward with information on three local men who had been lingering in the shadows close to the shop.

Yarham was brought back in for questioning and had hardly sat down before confessing to his part in the crime. He also implicated the three other men seen near the shop. James Mapes, John Hall and Robert Royal were marched into the station and, along with Yarham himself, charged with murder. The evidence was sparse to say the very least but the excitement emanating from the people of Great Yarmouth was inextinguishable.

The committal proceedings were dominated by Yarham's own testimony. He claimed to have heard noises downstairs on the night of the murder and on entering the shop, was confronted by Mapes, Hall and Royal. When he asked where Mrs Candler was he was told that she had been struck and was hidden behind the shop counter. Yarham had clearly placed himself at the scene of the crime whilst desperately trying to extricate himself from all liability. Unfortunately for him, the other three men all had alibis for the time of the attack. Witnesses came forward claiming Mapes, Hall and Royal were in the pub.

Yarham panicked. His story was flimsy and, unlike the other defendants, he had no one to back him up. In a desperate bid to wriggle out of his predicament he offered to turn Queen's Evidence. This, he believed, would ensure there could be no prosecution on his part during the trial. Unfortunately for him, he was wrong.

The trial itself took place in April 1845. Yarham had by this time become quite the celebrity and seemed positively happy to regale the jury with infinite details of the night in question. If anything, he appeared to know more now than at the time itself! However, on further questioning, Yarham's story began to unravel and he soon began to contradict his previous statements.

The trial lasted two days. The jury filed back into court after a very short period of deliberation only to announce a unanimous verdict of 'not guilty' for all three men. Sighs of relief all round for Mapes, Royal and Hall but Yarham was slightly less comfortable. The others were innocent men but he had claimed to be there himself and had no supporting witness to prove his inculpability.

A very sullied Yarham slunk out of the courtroom. The next few months were sheer hell for the fallen star witness. The local community yelled abuse and threatened him at every turn. Eventually he decided to leave Great Yarmouth and packed up for Gloucestershire but, being the slip-mouthed fool that he was, he confessed his part in the murder to a neighbour before leaving. As soon as he had left town the neighbour took this information straight to the local magistrate who called the police. Yarham, meanwhile, thought that his problems were over. He was convinced that he was untouchable now and without his abusive neighbours he could live a long and peaceful life.

It took the police a few months to track down a now complacent Samuel Yarham and bring him back to Great Yarmouth. The trial took place on 24th March 1846. Once again Yarham was the celebrity but this time in a more notorious capacity. Mrs Dick, the neighbour to whom Yarham had confided in, quietly told an astounded courtroom that it had been Yarham who had slit the throat of poor Harriet Candler, but only after Royal, Mapes and Hall had beaten her beyond recognition. He had killed her to put the woman out of her misery, or so he said. Silence fell upon those listening, for this information not only irrefutably implicated Yarham, it also meant that three guilty men had walked free from their trial. The jury took mere minutes to find Samuel Yarham guilty of the murder of Harriet Candler.

Two weeks later on 14th April, the man who had turned Queen's Evidence in the hopes of avoiding all liability, hanged from the gallows outside Norwich Castle. Had he not turned against his associates he would have almost certainly avoided the drop and been found not guilty. John Hall, Robert Royal and James Mapes watched their friend-turned traitor swing and then danced the night away at the Norwich fair.

Legal Ponderings - Turning 'Queen's Evidence'

'Turning Queen's Evidence' is a legal device whereby an accused or convicted criminal agrees to give useful information to either the police or to a court of law to help them catch other criminals. Occasionally the criminal testifies because of overwhelming guilt but this is extremely rare. More often than not, the prosecution or police will make an appealing offer in return for information. They might deliver a reduced sentence, place the defendant in a preferred prison location or, in very serious trials, offer to place the defendant in a Witness Protection Program.

If evidence in a violent criminal trial is flimsy and a conviction looks unlikely, the state may offer immunity from prosecution but this is not an automatic right to those turning Queen's Evidence. This, of course, was Samuel Yarham's fatal mistake. It could be argued that the prosecution should have made the situation clear to Yarham before the trial began and they certainly should have corrected his misinformed beliefs when they became apparent later on. However, this trial was not the first in which a lack of knowledge on the Defendant's part was used to the prosecution's advantage and it certainly was not the last.

Probably the most famous use of 'turning Queen's Evidence' in the United Kingdom was during the trial of Burke and Hare, the infamous Scottish Body Snatchers. William Hare was quick to turn against his best friend and accomplice, William Burke, in order to avoid the drop. He was given total immunity from prosecution and was said to have taken a seat right at the front of the baying crowds as his drinking buddy swung.

Chapter 12

The Landlord of the Lamb

Back in 1787 *Henry's Bar* in Norwich was known as the *Lamb Inn* and its landlord was one John Aggas. Fifty-one year old Aggas was an extremely popular gentleman, adored by the locals, especially the children who would visit the kindly landlord and listen to him telling wondrous stories whilst their parents socialised at the bar. His fame as a storyteller soon spread and people from all over Norfolk would travel to the Inn with their youngsters to hear tales of spooks and fairies.

John's brother-in-law, Thomas Hardy, had a less salubrious reputation and when he came to visit his sister, Aggas' wife, there was usually trouble. On 10th November 1787, Hardy and his wife made their way from Newton Flotman where they lived, with the intention of staying at the *Lamb Inn*. Before leaving, Hardy made a noticeable fuss regarding his favourite knife. He thought that he had lost it and refused to start the journey until it had been found. At his trial, Hardy's wife stated that she had no idea why her husband should have needed the knife but said that it was a treasured possession of his and that he did not like to be without it.

On their arrival, Mrs Hardy went up to her room whilst her husband made his way to the kitchens to speak with his sister. It did not take long for Hardy to start a fight, yelling and shouting in her face. John Aggas joined his wife and tried to calm the situation down. Thomas appeared to relax and even offered his hand to Aggas, claiming that he wanted no hard feelings between them. What happened next shocked all those in the kitchen who witnessed the event. As Hardy took John's hand and pulled him towards him, he drew out his knife and plunged it deep into Aggas' stomach. As John's knees began to buckle, Hardy ripped the knife upwards three or so inches. His intestines slithered out as he fell to the floor in a pool of his own blood. Mrs Aggas became understandably hysterical as the kitchen maid tried to pull her back from Hardy's reach.

Meanwhile, Hardy himself began to rant and rave about his own brother, John Hardy, claiming that if he were present at this moment he would stab him too. The man had completely lost control of his senses. As witnesses tried to overpower the madman he swung the knife back and forth until he turned it upon himself. His own wound was little more than a scratch and within a matter of moments he was tackled and dragged into a locked cupboard until the law arrived.

John Aggas was gently carried up to his room and cared for by the local Doctor and his wife but there was little to be done and by the following morning the old landlord was dead. Thomas Hardy was charged with his murder and taken to Norwich Castle to await his trial.

Joanna Elphick

At the start of the summer Assizes, Hardy was sentenced to hang. After the execution, his body was carried away and dissected by eager surgeons. Mrs Aggas could no longer stand to live at the *Lamb Inn* and so it was sold off to another family. She moved away and was never heard of again.

The new landlord and his family quickly settled into the Inn but almost straight away, strange events began to unfold. Echoing footsteps could be heard upstairs after everyone had gone home and the family were in bed. This was followed by knocking sounds coming from inside the walls. If the kitchen was left in a mess the night before, it would be clean and tidy the following day.

The children soon began to tell tales of a kindly old man that sat at the end of their beds during the night. He told them wonderful stories and kept them company until they drifted off to sleep. Such visitations have continued throughout the twentieth century. In 1978 two girls were invited upstairs whilst conducting some market research. An old man wandered past them, opening a door and shutting it behind him. Afterwards, the women packed their things away and knocked on the door to say goodbye. On opening the door they were astonished to find an empty cupboard and no more. He has, more recently, been seen on CCTV footage rocking in an old chair. Far from getting rid of his brother-in-law, Thomas Hardy's actions appear to have ensured that the old landlord would stay forever…

Chapter 13

The Abominable Sins of the Tailor of Diss

On Sunday 4th April 1742, nearly four thousand people stormed the churchyard in the usually sleepy market town of Diss in the hopes of catching sight of its most infamous villager. The following day a local tailor by the name of Robert Carlton was to be hanged on Diss Common for the shocking crimes of murder and sodomy but on this final day he was desperately trying to make his peace with God, cowering in the pews under the watchful eye of the local guards.

It had been common knowledge that Robert practiced the 'abominable sin' but whilst he kept himself to himself and worked hard, the locals tended to leave him be. He was a fine tailor and this undoubtedly helped him to avoid persecution. However, in 1735 Carlton took in a handsome young lodger by the name of John Lincoln. The two quickly became lovers, Robert falling deeply in love whilst John briefly enjoyed the secretive thrill. Unfortunately, whilst Carlton wallowed in the 'flesh-pots of Egypt' his lodger soon found the situation wearisome and he began to look elsewhere for fun.

A chance meeting with a young girl from Redgrave instigated a change of heart in John Lincoln. Mary Frost was a remarkably pretty and innocent maid: the complete antithesis of his middle-aged lover. In a rather callous manner Lincoln brought the girl back to his lodgings to show off his new sweetheart. Carlton raged at the impertinence and jealously threw Mary into the street. Once alone, he begged his former lover to come back to him but it was to no avail. John Lincoln was a man in love and he intended to marry the girl as soon as possible.

At this point something snapped inside Robert Carlton. Having audibly threatened to kill the girl if he got the chance, Carlton then became unnaturally calm and understanding. He appeared to quickly accept the change of circumstances, so much so that he even invited Mary and her landlord, Samuel Fuller, over for a cold supper.

On a murky November evening in 1741, Mary and Samuel made the journey to Robert's house. The beneficent host was all charm and cheer as he presented his guests with a juicy loin of mutton. Samuel was offered the salt first only to find there was very little left for the remaining guests. Mary was unperturbed by the lack of condiments but Carlton insisted on getting her some more. He quickly left the room and returned with a full salt pot which he shook liberally over her meal before settling down to his own unsalted mutton. The evening went well considering the awkward situation and the three agreed to share another supper before too long.

Samuel took Mary home and went straight to bed but was woken during the night by a dreadful moaning sound emanating from Mary's room. A doctor was called but little could be done to ease her pain. The poor girl died in unimaginable agony and after her death an autopsy showed that all internal organs had practically melted as a result of vast quantities of poison. Both a distraught John Lincoln and a horrified Samuel Fuller pointed the finger at Robert Carlton, who was immediately arrested and taken off to Thetford where he would stand trial at the following Assizes.

The trial itself was short but not particularly sweet. Evidence was overwhelming considering Carlton had bought a large quantity of 'Sublimate of Mercury' from an apothecary the day before and had declared his hatred of Mary Frost on numerous occasions. Although he could have been convicted of sodomy at any point during his adult life, the community had turned a blind eye. But since his homosexual jealousy had resulted in the death of an innocent young woman, the general ambivalence towards his sexual conduct had mutated into utter loathing and disgust. Carlton stood no chance of avoiding the death sentence.

Spectators poured forth from every corner of the region in the hope of catching sight of the despicable tailor of Diss. Various bizarre occurrences were set up for the pleasure of the ever-growing crowds; the first being Carlton's opportunity to repent in church. The second oddity occurred in the nearby public house where Robert and John were forced to meet and drink one last ale together. A symbolic sharing of biscuits proved to the onlookers that the once lovers parted as friends. But the main event was, of course, the hanging itself. There had been no executions in Diss in living memory and new gallows were quickly erected upon the common on the outskirts of the town. A gibbet was also hastily raised in anticipation of its most infamous inhabitant.

It was mid-afternoon when a sorrowful Robert Carlton was driven to the Common in an open cart. When offered the chance to confess he vehemently denied murdering Mary Frost but made no such comment with regard to his sexual dalliance. After the execution, his body was carried back to the site of the murder and in a gruesome display of unseemliness, the corpse was hung up in the middle of the room and gawkers charged two pence a peek.

Finally Carlton was left to rot on in the gibbet, swinging in the breeze until the crows finally picked his bones clean.

Legal Ponderings - Criminal Offence of Homosexuality

Undoubtedly Samuel Carlton's private life was an integral factor in the automatic assumption of guilt on the part of the Thetford court and the ensuing reaction of the people of Diss. Anal intercourse was identified as an offence punishable by hanging under the Buggery Act of 1533 and the death penalty was not removed for homosexuality until 1861. However, such homosexual acts remained illegal and were, in fact, widened to include any sexual acts between males.

On 3rd September 1957 the Wolfenden Report was published recommending that 'homosexual behaviour between consenting adults in private should no longer be a criminal offence.' After many notable individuals spoke up in favour of decriminalising homosexuality the Sexual Offences Act was finally passed in 1967 for those of twenty-one years of age and over. In 2001 the age of consent was brought in line with heterosexual individuals through the Sexual Offences (Amendment) Act. Since then homosexual rights have gathered momentum and now include the right to change legal gender, joint and step-child adoptions and, of course, the introduction of Civil Partnerships and same-sex marriage.

Nobody openly mourned or defended Samuel Carlton. Provocation was a much-used defence for those who lost their minds over the infidelity of a loved one but this did not stretch to homosexual relationships. There were undoubtedly other practicing homosexuals in the town of Diss at the time of the execution, and as Oscar Wilde once said:

And alien tears will fill for him
Pity's long-broken urn,
For his mourners will be outcast men,
And outcasts always mourn.

Chapter 14

Marriage, Madness, Murder & Suicide

When Louis Thain married Fanny Chadd on 20th March 1905, no one could have guessed the ghastly end resulting from such a union.

Forty-two year old widow Fanny Chadd was a quiet woman with an impressive figure and an equally impressive bank balance. Whether it was her ample curves or her bulging purse that caught Louis Thain's eye, who could say but he quickly began to court the woman and it was not long before he proposed.

Mrs Chadd, however, was extremely wary of her new beau's advances since her husband's will made it perfectly clear that should she remarry, one third of her late husband's bequest would be lost to her forever. When she explained her predicament to Louis he merely shrugged. He was, after all, an independently wealthy man. If she married him he would automatically reimburse her for her lost money. She would

Joanna Elphick

be financially independent and emotionally supported. What could be nicer?

Unfortunately Mr Louis Thain was a liar - an impoverished liar to boot! It wasn't long into the marriage that Thain had guzzled away the house keeping and Fanny soon realised that any money her husband might have once owned had evaporated along with his charm and thoughtful disposition. Louis Thain was a drunken, violent bully and Fanny had rapidly become his proverbial punch bag.

By October 1908, their financial situation was looking bleak. Thain somehow convinced Fanny to place the last of the money into a hotel lease in Kings Lynn. Reluctantly, she complied and the pair began setting up a new business. Initially, things began to pick up and, as the money increased the quarrelling subsided but it was not Thain's natural state to work hard and he soon lost interest in the running of the hotel. Before too long Fanny was left to cook, clean, do the accounts and generally run the business. Busy days turned into busy weeks, starting at dawn and continuing way into the night. With no help whatsoever from her errant husband it was inevitable that Fanny was to overreach herself. Thain staggered home one evening to find his wife collapsed upon the floor. Doctors announced that she was physically exhausted and as a result spent the following nine weeks in hospital.

A rejuvenated Mrs Thain returned to a ransacked Hotel. The rooms had clearly been overturned and the linen had all been pawned. Fanny had no option but to foreclose on the lease, thereby losing over £300 in the process.

Within two years she had lost her business and her money. The quiet, unassuming widow of independent means was now reduced to rented rooms in Cleveland Road, Lowestoft. As the money dwindled, the beatings increased. However, Fanny was a quick-witted woman and soon came up with the notion of taking in a lodger to supplement their earnings.

Mr Frederick William Davis was a retired musician who had been unwell for some time. Moving in with Mrs Thain was an obvious blessing for them both since they gave one another companionship and a friendly ear. Louis, of course, was instantly fired up with jealousy and hatred. Having accused the couple of having an affair he proceeded to make Davis' life unbearable. Whenever Davis attempted to play his piano, Thain would smash crockery at the walls and bang a broom upon the ceiling in order to put him off. As the violence escalated between the warring couple, the exhausted lodger became increasingly distressed. The final straw occurred one afternoon when Davis returned home only to find Mrs Thain lying on the kitchen floor, Louis Thain kneeling on her chest with a knife to her throat. Fanny had simply refused to hand over any more money for him to go drinking. Davis begged Fanny to leave and then promptly took his own advice. Her friend and only source of income disappeared simultaneously with the slamming of the front door.

Louis also left the house in a fit of pique, declaring that the marriage was over. Of course this did not stop the violent assaults. Various humiliating incidents transpired both behind closed doors and in front of others, such as her very dear friend Mrs Bewley and her daughter, Ethel, who witnessed Thain throwing bottles at Fanny. On this particular occasion the police were called and Louis was

Joanna Elphick

escorted off the premises. Fanny Thain finally came to her senses and decided to divorce her cruel husband. Mrs Bewley was delighted and both mother and daughter quickly took their friend in until the divorce hearing. It was a terrifying time for the three women, who were systematically victimized by an increasingly unhinged Thain.

Their fear would undoubtedly have increased exponentially had they known that Louis had taken a trip to Great Yarmouth where he had used a fraudulent license to purchase a gun. The illegal weapon was carefully taken back to his lodgings and hidden until its great unveiling.

Eventually the court hearing rolled round and on Thursday 10th July, a number of witnesses were brought forward to testify against Louis Thain's cruelty towards Fanny. Much to their discomfort, Thain sat in the back row of the court during the proceedings smiling as each witness was called to the stand.

It soon became clear that Louis Thain was unstable and, more importantly, an unfit husband. The magistrate found in favour of Fanny Thain, granting her the divorce and passing all costs on to Mr Thain. The entire court solemnly watched as Thain left the court house, a minacious smirk upon his face. Frederick Davis, knowing Thain's vicious demeanour better than most, offered to walk both Fanny and the Bewley ladies back home. However, even he did not imagine the ferocious attack that was about to be unleashed upon them.

The group had hardly got out of sight of the Magistrates court when Thain leapt out of an alleyway, brandishing his newly acquired gun. He wildly fired at Mrs Bewley as she turned and ran in fear. The bullet passed her but unfortunately hit her daughter, Ethel, who fell to the floor with a wounded arm. Davis grabbed a shocked Fanny by the hand and proceeded to pull her down the street and round the corner. As the frightened woman turned to look over her shoulder, a second bullet was fired and struck her full in the face. Fanny lay motionless upon the floor and Davis understandably thought his friend was dead. Galvanised by sheer fear, Davis continued to run. Thain was also under the assumption that he had killed his wife and so he stepped over her still body and continued on his murderous rampage. In fact the bullet had struck Fanny, slicing through her face but coming out the other side. Although she was badly wounded, she had merely fainted.

Mr Arthur Myhill was eating his lunch with his wife when the second shot was fired and came outside to find poor Fanny Thain crumpled on the pavement at his front gate. His wife immediately attended to the unconscious woman whilst Arthur chased after Thain and Davis. It soon became clear that Frederick Davis was in mortal danger as his assailant was fast catching up and so Arthur Myhill called out a warning. It was an extremely brave but ultimately a fatal move to make. Thain turned and fired, hitting Myhill directly in the chest. He died instantly.

By this time the police had also joined the chase and as they moved in Thain realised that the game was over. Davis was dragged into a front garden and Thain was left out in the street surrounded by policemen. As they closed in on their fugitive, Thain turned the gun upon himself, lodging a bullet in his brain.

Both Fanny Thain and Ethel Bewley survived their tragic ordeal, testifying at the posthumous trial of Louis Thain. Ultimately, he was found guilty of the wilful murder of Arthur Myhill and in an unpleasant quirk of fate Arthur's body was buried no more than a few feet away from his killer in Lowestoft Cemetery.

One solitary clergyman and the undertaker stood by the coffin as Thain was laid to rest. His overwhelming fear of being alone had finally come true.

Chapter 15

The Last Dance of Louie Bryant

It seems most fitting that this book should end just as it began, with a couple of unsolved mysteries...

On an overcast Friday night in late September, 1829, the residents of Diss congregated in an old barn nestled between the Baptist Church and a wooden post-mill for a celebratory dance. The Royal Sessions had just finished and everybody was in a joyous mood despite the threatening storm clouds. None more so, it had to be said, than young Louie Bryant, a separated wife and notorious good-time girl. Louie was a gregarious, bubbly creature who loved to meet up with her friends and dance the night away. Since her husband had walked out some years previously and made his way to London, the abandoned wife had not wasted time mourning her loss. Instead, the suddenly independent woman revelled in her newfound situation.

As the rain lashed against the barn door, those inside whirled and jigged to the frantic fiddles and shared the freely flowing ale. Everybody was in high spirits. However,

Joanna Elphick

during the festivities a stranger appeared at the barn door asking after young Louie Bryant. The girl was spotted and beckoned over, whereupon the two moved into the shadows and began an animated discussion. Moments later, the unknown gentleman slipped out through the door and back into the stormy darkness. Seconds later, a preoccupied Louie waved goodbye to her friends and without a word she too disappeared, never to be seen alive again.

It was not until the following morning that poor Louie Bryant was discovered. Her blood-soaked clothes wrapped a pitiful corpse, mutilated and tossed to the ground like a grotesque ragdoll. She had barely made it out of earshot when her killer had attacked. Having repeatedly stabbed her he made his escape across the fields, leaving the murder weapon in a muddy plough furrow.

As by now you are more than aware, the unearthing of a bona fide murder causes a certain frisson throughout the local population and Diss was no exception. The people were horrified that such an atrocity could have occurred within their God-fearing community. Although some could not help but turn the sorry tale into a warning against loose living - live well and purely, live long and safely under the watchful eyes of God. Young Louie Bryant had lived a little too well and look where that had got her!

The recovered knife held no clues whatsoever and was quickly discarded. The clothing, however, was another matter entirely. The slashed and bloody material was of great interest to those investigating the crime, but when this yielded no more information than that she had fought bravely, the dress and cloak took on a new role as a macabre curiosity for paying gawkers. The exhibition proved extremely profitable and remained on view for a number of decades before finally being burnt.

The stranger was obviously the prime suspect and was quickly hunted down. Interestingly, the investigators immediately believed his story of an unknown gentleman who bribed him into giving Ms Bryant a secret note and he was released. The absent husband was also 'of interest', but having been brought back from London to testify he too was released since he had a firm alibi at the time of the killing. Other suspects came and went, each with their own excuse, alibi or witness absolving them of all guilt.

The ghastly death of pretty, vivacious Louie Bryant has never been solved and her sorrowful ghost is said to wander along the path, now commonly known as Louie's Lane.

Chapter 16

All's Well That Ends Well

My last offering is one based on gossip and hearsay but one thing is undeniably true; the murdered body of a young maidservant lies in the churchyard of Steeple Morden and her killers were never brought to justice.

The infamous Moco Farm, now demolished, received a great deal of unwanted publicity during its time looming over Cheyney Water. Tales of ghostly screams and wailing spirits were recorded as far back as 1901 in the *Royston Crow*, a local newspaper, when the gamekeeper, his wife and a shepherd by the name of Levett all heard ungodly sounds from within. Further witnesses confirmed the haunting which, according to the *Crow*, caused 'a great sensation in the village'. However, the real crimes occurred far earlier and were far more terrifying.

In 1734 a local farmer and his wife successfully ran Moco Farm, employing a number of servants and farm-hands. Their maidservant was an eighteen-year-old girl by the name of Elizabeth Pateman. John Pateman, her father, was known to have been extremely proud of his daughter due to her goodly position at the farm where she 'lived in'.

It was during the wintry month of February that a travelling pedlar visited Steeple Morden. The villagers were kind to the old man, sharing bread and offering board. As a result his face quickly became known. He was last seen heading towards Moco Farm, claiming that surely there he would be able to sell his wares and make some money for the journey onwards. His promise to say goodbye before moving on was never fulfilled for, although he was seen arriving at the farmstead, he was never seen leaving.

At this point the rumours began. Locals soon claimed that someone up at the farm had 'done the old boy in' and the wealthy farmer and his wife were prime suspects. Further reports emerged that not only had the pedlar disappeared, but also all the farm-hands had been expressly forbidden to use the well. Apparently the water had stagnated and the farmer quickly filled the well in. Clearly not enough to hang a man but more than enough to raise a few eyebrows.

It was at this time that a second incident occurred. Elizabeth's beau stated on record that she had called him into the farmhouse one afternoon and told him that she had a secret to share, a very serious secret. When the boy had begged her to tell him more there and then, she had refused, saying she didn't want to be overheard since the mistress of the house was only in the next room. He was never to see Elizabeth alive again and it is at this juncture that fact and fiction cannot be separated. The truth will almost certainly never be discovered.

What we can be sure of is that the following day Elizabeth Pateman was discovered inside the farm house, her mutilated corpse lying on the ground. The body was found by the master of the house, James Hoy, who claimed that he had heard the young girl groaning at about five o'clock in the morning and, rushing down to see what the matter was, stumbled upon the gruesome sight. The *British Observator* of Saturday 15th March 1734 gave a vivid account of the scene. Upon entering the room he 'found her on the floor all over blood, her check bone broke, a large piece of flesh cut out of her neck in the jugular vein, and miserably bruis'd in other parts of the body.' A casement window had carefully been removed from the south side of the house along with a small iron bar, leaving a hole just big enough to let the killer in. Burglary was clearly not a motive since seven silver spoons had been left untouched on the sideboard. Strangely, three untapped bottles of ale had been taken from the cellar and left in the yard. Curiouser and curiouser! Suspicion initially landed firmly on the broken-hearted sweetheart who, it was thought, had taken advantage of the innocent girl and then killed her to hide his wicked secret. The boy vehemently denied the accusations. A surgeon was called in to examine poor Elizabeth and it was quickly established the she had died 'in her innocency'. At this point the Justices of the Peace were at a loss. They had discovered a coulter, a knife-like implement used to clear the point of the plough share, at the scene of the crime but this yielded no clues. A pea hook and penknife were also thought to have been used upon the body but, yet again, held no clues as to the killer's identity. The final judgement was weak to say the very least. Their general conclusion was that 'she had been privy to some Male-practices in a person thereabouts who had but an indifferent character, and for fear of discovery he thought fit to remove her out of the way.' The villagers were suitably unimpressed and it wasn't long before more damning versions bubbled to the surface. The pedlar's disappearance had all but been forgotten in the hullaballoo but suddenly the event took on new and even more sinister dimensions. Not only had the farmer and his wife killed the pedlar and thrown him down the well, they had also surely murdered their maidservant to silence her once and for all. The mistress had obviously overheard Elizabeth talking to her sweetheart and, knowing the dark secret she intended to tell him, got her husband to cut her down. The window was removed to suggest an outsider had committed the crime and the murder weapons left in full view suggesting sudden flight. They were, of course, pieces of equipment used by the farmhands on a daily basis.

The story is plausible but not exactly concrete. Nobody liked James Hoy and his wife. They were, after all, very wealthy at a time when the rest of the community was struggling but I'm not convinced successful farming automatically suggests they were capable of multiple murders. However, one thing is certain; somebody killed Elizabeth Pateman in an extremely vicious attack. Bizarrely, her grave became a notorious landmark since it was decorated with the implements of her death: the coulter, the pen knife and the pea hook. Gruesome in the extreme! Beneath the carving lies a poem:

Here lies interred a harmless maid,
By cruel hands to death betrayed
And though the murder is concealed on earth
In heaven it is revealed.
And they who did it soon shall know,

Joanna Elphick

The righteous judge sees all below.
Therefore repent whoe'er you be.
Or I'll foretell your destiny.
In Hell's dark furnace dark and deep,
Your wretched soul shall wail and weep.
While she, I hope, in heaven on high,
Shall live above the lofty sky.

So ends the sorry tale of young Elizabeth Pateman. Although the carvings are no longer visible upon the tombstone due to time and weather erosion, her pitiful ghost is often said to wander the churchyard, wringing her hands and sobbing forlornly, waiting for justice to be done.

The grave of Elizabeth Pateman.

Chapter 17

And So to Bed...

It is really rather nice curling up in bed with a good book, especially one bursting with murder, mayhem, intrigue and horror. Hopefully this tome (pardon the pun) has ticked most of these boxes for you but actually, there is something even better than reading about such tales and flicking through the photographs. Better by far to explore the sights for yourself.

Some of the tales that I have shared with you have left little of themselves upon the landscape whilst others have positively stained their surroundings. It is extremely exciting to trace the last footsteps of the victim or linger by the graveside of some poor soul that you have just read about.

Should you wish to walk the dark paths of murderous East Anglia, may I suggest two particularly fruitful locations: the first is Peasenhall, such a beautiful village where you can easily walk past Providence House and gaze up into the very window that Rose Harsent left a candle burning on that fateful night. Her grave can also be found, although this is harder to spot.

The second, and possibly most rewarding site to visit, is Polstead, another magnificent Suffolk village. Here, much evidence can be found of its ghastly past. Maria Marten's cottage and Corder House can be viewed from the road, along with Maria's wooden marker in the graveyard. The Red Barn no longer stands but you can walk through the field where she scurried to her death.

Visiting the sites for yourself is a fascinating and deeply rewarding hobby but be warned! Some locals do not wish to associate themselves with their hometown's sordid past and, if you should want to take a peek, please remember to mind individuals' privacy. Their homes are not public museums and they may not wish to consider its darker history. Use your imagination, wander through the lonely byways and wooded paths, but may I suggest you don't go alone. After all, that is how those who walked before made it into my book.

The End

Murderous East Anglia

Cheyney Water

A Final Thank You

Before you shut this book and rush off to explore the darker side of East Anglia for yourself, I would ask that you let me share with you a very heart-felt thank you to some very special people.

Firstly, my parents, who positively encouraged my macabre fascination with all things murderous as a child and dutifully shuttled me around the county as I shared my findings with like-minded souls through lectures and after dinner speeches. I would not have even considered this project without you.

Similarly, my husband, who never questioned why I needed to root around graveyards from one side of the county to the other, torch in hand and umbrella over my head, you just found the appropriate map and whisked me to my desired destination. A genuine adventurer and a real trooper to boot!

Finally, my boys. Toby, you have grown up as wonderfully warped as I and I know you will be the very first to read this book. Your unwavering belief in all I do means everything to me. Rufus, you faithfully follow your mad mother in rain or shine, holding notebooks, poking about where you know you shouldn't and, most of all, taking some outstanding photographs for this book. Your well-crafted shots bring my words to life.

To you all,
Thank you
xxx